The State of the World Atlas

The State of the World Atlas

Michael Kidron & Ronald Segal

A Pluto Press project

Simon & Schuster   New York

Published by Simon and Schuster
A Division of Gulf & Western Corporation
Simon & Schuster Building
Rockefeller Center
1230 Avenue of the Americas
New York, New York 10020

SIMON AND SCHUSTER and colophon
are trade marks of Simon & Schuster

Artwork for maps by Swanston & Associates, Derby, England
Layout and other design by Marsha Austin
Editor and production coordinator Anne Benewick

Introduction and notes typeset by
Latimer Trend & Company Ltd., Plymouth, England
Printed in Hong Kong

4 5 6 7 8 9 10

Library of Congress Catalog Card No 80-5921

ISBN 0 671 42438 6
      0 671 42439 4 Pbk.

Contents

Introduction

The Aggressive State

1. The State by Geography
2. The Proliferation of States
3. The State by Population
4. The State Invades Antarctica
5. The States Invades the Sea
6. Invasions of the Sky

Arms and the State

7. Foreign Military Presence
8. Military Spending
9. The Nuclear Club
10. Air Power
11. Arms for the Sake of the Profit
12. States at War in the 1970s

Natural Resources

13. Mineral Power
14. The World Mineral Powers
15. Energy Power
16. Oil Power
17. Nuclear Power
18. Food Power

Economy

19. Industrial Power

20. Technological Power
21. Dependence and Diversity
22. Trade Power
23. National Income
24. The Debt-Laden South
25. Margins of Safety

Government

26. Government Income
27. The State Apparatus
28. Military Government
29. Bullets and Blackboards
30. Conscription and Conscience
31. Scourges of the State
32. Refugees

Holds on the Mind

33. Languages of Rule
34. Religions of Rule

Business

35. The Public and the Private
36. The Nationality of Transnationals
37. The Islands of the Blessed

Labour

38. The Flight to Work
39. Exploitation

40. The Labour Force
41. Women Workers
42. The Force of Labour

Society

43. Rich and Poor People
44. Our Daily Bread
45. Bill of Health
46. The Right to Learn
47. The Longer Reach
48. Holes in the Safety Net
49. The Swelling Cities
50. Slumland
51. Law and Disorder
52. The Unemployment Time Bomb

Environment

53. Fouling the Nest
54. The Dying Earth

Symptoms of Crisis

55. Industrial Droop
56. The First Inflationary Crest, 1974
57. Funny Money
58. Credit Runs Riot
59. Panic Stations

Signs of Dissent

60. Nuclear Power No Thanks
61. Nationalism Against the Nation State
62. Russia's Ununited Republics
63. 'Our Bodies Our Selves'
64. The Student Sixties
65. Urban Heavings in the Seventies

66. Worldrise

The States of the World

Notes on the Maps

Subject Index

Introduction

The State of the World Atlas stems from the rich tradition of political atlases, born out of war or the threat of war, and out of the widespread interest that this excited in military strategy and deployment. In time the tradition came to embrace economic, social and cultural factors; reflecting and promoting the diffusion of knowledge about the world at large which has accompanied the spread of mass education, new forms of communication and international travel.

Like the others in their time, this atlas seeks to fulfil a need for information and interpretation. It identifies the major topics of public concern. It provides a frame of reference for the changing pattern of events. It explains connections that are obscure in themselves or have been deliberately obscured. And it does all this as graphically as possible, in our belief that the information so provided is more easily grasped in this way than through texts and tables.

But this atlas does rather more than its predecessors. It endeavours to be truly international: not only in showing the world-wide incidence of this or that condition or event, but in associating that incidence with an underlying structure – the self-perpetuating system of sovereign states preoccupied with aggrandisement and conflict. While it is true that the state has in its time been an instrument for the extension of personal liberty and for much material progress, it has also been an instrument of personal oppression, collective violence and economic waste. It is our contention that the destructive aspects of the state have come crucially to exceed the constructive ones.

The first section of this atlas shows how states have proliferated in the last few decades and how, with their rival claims, they are reaching out to possess the last uninhabited land mass, the high seas and the sky. The maps then turn to the military preoccupations of the state and the squandering of resources on war, the threat of war, and preparations to meet the threat of war.

The power of states rests on more than arms alone. We show how unequally states are endowed with natural and developed resources, how they employ those endowments and how they are related to the power of private industry and finance. We then consider the impact of all this on labour, on society in general and on the environment, before tracing the symptoms of crisis and identifying some of the mounting challenges to the system.

The great mass of information presented in these maps comes from governments and international agencies, whose statistics often constitute the only available source. Some states, lacking the means or the will to provide accurate statistics, may have published mere approximations – as for infant mortality rates, used in *Map 45: Bill of Health* which contain substantial ingredients of wishful thinking. In other cases, states provide no information at all, or may refuse to make public information they plainly have. The USSR and related states, for example, do not reveal figures for gold and foreign currency reserves. And in some cases, information for some states could be obtained only on a basis which would encourage misleading comparisons. In many of these, we have preferred to leave gaps.

On the understanding that all statistics may be suspect, we have used in this atlas those that we believe are valid enough for broad comparison. Band sizes have been adopted and moving averages used both to isolate certain trends and to reduce dependence on the accuracy of particular statistics. Where possible, the extreme range of statistical events has been given in the keys to the maps. And if reservations are still considered necessary, these are made in the relevant notes.

Some statistics had to be rejected altogether, a fact best exemplified by *Map 52: The Unemployment Time Bomb*, for which an International Labour Office projection was eventually used, in the form of a chart. Not only do the official unemployment rates reported by many poor states bear no recognizable relation to reality, but the existence, reported to us, of strictly confidential and alarming statistics for unemployment in advanced industrial states, confirmed our already deep suspicion of even the best figures publicly provided.

Some generally accepted statistics are marred by conceptual flaws. Gross national product (GNP) is a common measure and is used in several maps. Yet in largely agricultural societies it conveys only roughly, if at all, the value of subsistence production; and in largely industrialized societies it ignores the value of the domestic labour that confines the lives of so many women. Because it involves the use of a national currency, currently the US dollar, as an international standard, it requires further qualification. Even under conditions of monetary stability, a national currency is significantly affected by both the performance of the related national economy and by shifts in international investment. In a period of floating exchange rates, when the value of the dollar standard in other currencies moves constantly and often sharply, the distortions are enormous.

Two further observations on the use of statistics are necessary. That the very choice of which figures to collect must involve the bias of those who choose them may be exemplified by *Map 45: Bill of Health*. The provision of hospital beds is a measure of medical care that ignores traditional forms of medical treatment, available in many societies, but for which there is no statistical index. The availability of information also imposed limitations. Whereas we had hoped to include a map on the progress of the movement for women's liberation, we had to limit ourselves for lack of a more explicit measure to a comparison of abortion rights (see *Map 63: 'Our Bodies Our Selves'*).

In a number of instances, maps have been based on a degree of personal judgement. For example, information for *Map 42: The Force of Labour*, came out of intensive discussions with leading international trade union officials. Wherever possible, their judgement was checked by others. On occasion, however (for example *Map 28: Military Government* and *Map 34: Religions of Rule*), we had to fall back on our own assessment, in the light of incomplete, ambiguous or contradictory information.

Some maps, such as *Map 64: The Student Sixties* or *Map 65: Urban Heavings in the Seventies*, are the result of extensive culling of newspaper reports. And still others have been augmented in this way: *Map 32: Refugees* or *Map 44: Our Daily Bread*. Such a method presents practical limitations and had to be confined to newspapers in the major European languages.

The projection used throughout is Winkel's Tripel, an 'equal-area' projection which provides a familiar view of our spherical world. For reasons of space and scale, and because detailed information is rarely available for them, some tiny island states appear on very few maps, notably *Map 2: The Proliferation of States*, and *Map 5: The State Invades the Sea*. State boundaries conform to those used in *The Times Atlas of the World*. State names have been given on the maps in their shorter and more commonly used form: for full designations, see the list of states which follows the maps.

A project such as this could not have made the journey from concept to publication without help from many people and their resources of energy, knowledge and talent. We must, first and foremost, thank Anne Benewick, our editor, creative intermediary and production coordinator at Pluto Press. We must thank Malcolm Swanston of Swanston & Associates, who prepared the artwork for the maps, and Marsha Austin who prepared the layouts, for their keen understanding of our purposes, their inventiveness and skills. We must thank Nina Kidron of Pluto Press whose judgement and ingenuity were crucial to the publication. And we must thank Richard Kuper of Pluto Press and David Kewley of Pan Books for their continued advice and support.

    Too many people, in too many places to be listed, have responded readily to requests for guidance, information and reassurance. We are grateful to all of them. And, not least, we wish to thank each other, for mutual encouragement and understanding.

Michael Kidron
Ronald Segal
August 1980

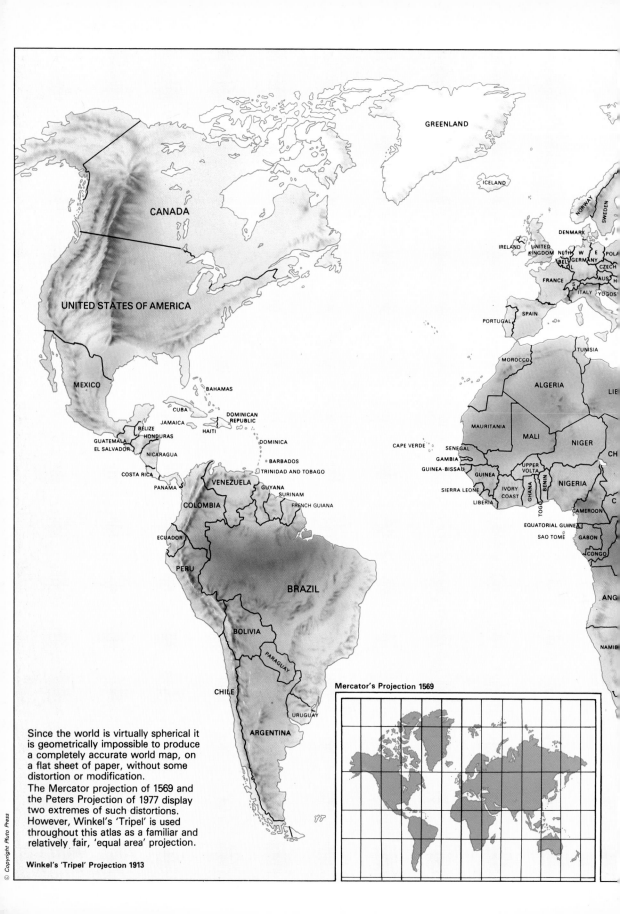

GREENLAND

ICELAND

CANADA

NORWAY
SWEDEN
DENMARK
IRELAND UNITED
KINGDOM NETH
BEL GERMANY
FRANCE CZECH
AUS H
S ITALY YUGOS

UNITED STATES OF AMERICA

PORTUGAL SPAIN

MEXICO

BAHAMAS

TUNISIA

MOROCCO

ALGERIA

LIE

CUBA

DOMINICAN
REPUBLIC

JAMAICA

BELIZE
HONDURAS

HAITI

GUATEMALA
EL SALVADOR

NICARAGUA

DOMINICA

COSTA RICA

BARBADOS

PANAMA

TRINIDAD AND TOBAGO

VENEZUELA

GUYANA
SURINAM

COLOMBIA

FRENCH GUIANA

ECUADOR

PERU

BRAZIL

MAURITANIA

MALI

NIGER

CAPE VERDE

SENEGAL

GAMBIA

GUINEA-BISSAU

SIERRA LEONE

GUINEA

LIBERIA

IVORY
COAST

UPPER
VOLTA

GHANA

BENIN

NIGERIA

TOGO

CH

C

CAMEROON

EQUATORIAL GUINEA

SAO TOME

GABON

CONGO

ANG

BOLIVIA

PARAGUAY

NAMIB

CHILE

URUGUAY

ARGENTINA

Mercator's Projection 1569

Since the world is virtually spherical it
is geometrically impossible to produce
a completely accurate world map, on
a flat sheet of paper, without some
distortion or modification.
The Mercator projection of 1569 and
the Peters Projection of 1977 display
two extremes of such distortions.
However, Winkel's 'Tripel' is used
throughout this atlas as a familiar and
relatively fair, 'equal area' projection.

Winkel's 'Tripel' Projection 1913

UNION OF SOVIET SOCIALIST REPUBLICS

MONGOLIA

TURKEY

CYPRUS
SYRIA
LEBANON
ISRAEL
JORDAN
IRAQ
IRAN
AFGHANISTAN

KUWAIT

BAHRAIN
QATAR
UAE
OMAN

PAKISTAN

N
KOREA
S

JAPAN

CHINA

BHUTAN
NEPAL

TAIWAN

HONG KONG

EGYPT

SAUDI ARABIA

N
S YEMEN
YEMEN
DJIBOUTI

SUDAN

ETHIOPIA

SOMALIA

UGANDA
KENYA

RWANDA
BURUNDI

TANZANIA

COMOROS

MALAWI

MBABWE

MOZAMBIQUE

MADAGASCAR

INDIA

B-
DESH

BURMA

LAOS

VIETNAM

THAILAND

KAM

PHILIPPINES

SRI LANKA

BRUNEI

MALAYSIA

SINGAPORE

INDONESIA

KIRIBATI
(GILBERT ISLANDS)

PAPUA
NEW GUINEA

H
S
A

Peters' Projection 1977

AUSTRALIA

NEW ZEALAND

GREENLAND

ICELAND

NORWAY SWEDEN

CANADA

DENMARK

IRELAND UNITED
KINGDOM

W E
GERMANY CZE
AUS
FRANCE
ITALY YUG

PORTUGAL SPAIN

UNITED STATES OF AMERICA

TUNISIA

MOROCCO

ALGERIA L

MEXICO

BAHAMAS

DOMINICAN REPUBLIC
PUERTO RICO
VIRGIN ISLANDS, BRITISH
ST. CHRISTOPHER ANTIGUA
(KITTS)-NEVIS-ANGUILLA GUADELOUPE
DOMINICA
MARTINIQUE
ST. LUCIA
ST. VINCENT BARBADOS
GRENADA
TOBAGO
VENEZUELA TRINIDAD

MAURITANIA MALI NIGER

CUBA

DOMINICAN
REPUBLIC
BELIZE JAMAICA HAITI
GUATEMALA HONDURAS
EL SALVADOR
NICARAGUA

CAPE VERDE

SENEGAL
GAMBIA
GUINEA-BISSAU
GUINEA

UPPER
VOLTA

NIGERIA

COSTA RICA
PANAMA

BARBADOS

TRINIDAD AND TOBAGO

VENEZUELA GUYANA
SURINAM
FRENCH GUIANA

SIERRA LEONE
LIBERIA

IVORY
COAST

GHANA
TOGO
BENIN

CAMEROON

EQUATORIAL GUINEA
SAO TOME

GABON
CONGO

COLOMBIA

ECUADOR

FRANCE
ANDORRA
SPAIN

PERU

BRAZIL

AN

AUSTRIA
SWITZERLAND LIECHTENSTEIN

BOLIVIA

PARAGUAY

FRANCE
MONACO

CHILE

States with a population less than Cape Town
(around 1 million)

NAM

ITALY
SAN MARINO

URUGUAY

ARGENTINA

Bahamas	Luxembourg
Bahrain	Maldives
Barbados	Malta
Botswana	Mauritius
Brunei	Nauru
Cape Verde	Oman
Comoros	Qatar
Cyprus	Reunion
Djibouti	Sao Tomé and Principe
Dominica	Seychelles
Equatorial Guinea	Solomon Islands
Fiji	St. Vincent
Gabon	Surinam
Gambia	Swaziland
Grenada	Tuvalu
Guinea-Bissau	United Arab Emirates
Guyana	Western Samoa
Iceland	
Kiribati	

ROME
VATICAN CITY

FALKLAND ISLANDS

States independent before 1945

States independent since 1945

Colonies and other non-independent territories

Source: Statesman's Yearbook

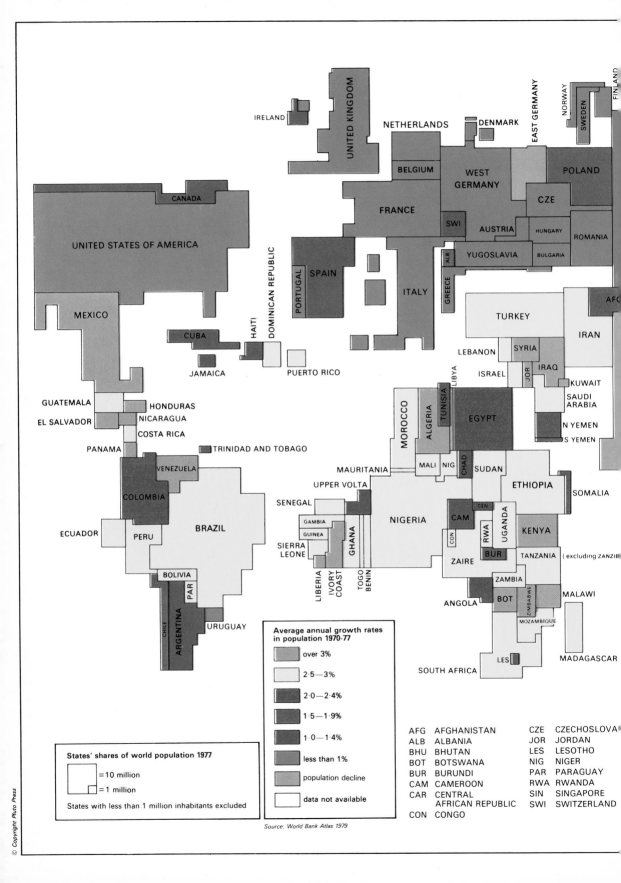

IRELAND
UNITED KINGDOM
NETHERLANDS
DENMARK
EAST GERMANY
NORWAY
SWEDEN
FINLAND
BELGIUM
WEST GERMANY
POLAND
FRANCE
CZE
SWI
AUSTRIA
HUNGARY
ROMANIA
ALB
YUGOSLAVIA
BULGARIA
PORTUGAL
SPAIN
ITALY
GREECE
TURKEY
AFG
IRAN
LEBANON
SYRIA
JOR
IRAQ
ISRAEL
KUWAIT
SAUDI ARABIA
N YEMEN
S YEMEN

CANADA
UNITED STATES OF AMERICA
MEXICO
DOMINICAN REPUBLIC
HAITI
CUBA
PUERTO RICO
JAMAICA
GUATEMALA
HONDURAS
EL SALVADOR
NICARAGUA
COSTA RICA
PANAMA
TRINIDAD AND TOBAGO
VENEZUELA
COLOMBIA
ECUADOR
PERU
BRAZIL
BOLIVIA
PAR
CHILE
ARGENTINA
URUGUAY

LIBYA
MOROCCO
ALGERIA
TUNISIA
EGYPT
MALI
NIG
CHAD
SUDAN
ETHIOPIA
SOMALIA
MAURITANIA
UPPER VOLTA
SENEGAL
GAMBIA
GUINEA
GHANA
NIGERIA
CEN
CAM
UGANDA
KENYA
SIERRA LEONE
CON
RWA
BUR
TANZANIA
(excluding ZANZIB
LIBERIA
IVORY COAST
TOGO
BENIN
ZAIRE
ZAMBIA
ANGOLA
BOT
ZIMBABWE
MALAWI
MOZAMBIQUE
LES
MADAGASCAR
SOUTH AFRICA

Average annual growth rates in population 1970-77

- over 3%
- 2·5—3%
- 2·0—2·4%
- 1·5—1·9%
- 1·0—1·4%
- less than 1%
- population decline
- data not available

States' shares of world population 1977

= 10 million
= 1 million

States with less than 1 million inhabitants excluded

AFG	AFGHANISTAN	CZE	CZECHOSLOVA
ALB	ALBANIA	JOR	JORDAN
BHU	BHUTAN	LES	LESOTHO
BOT	BOTSWANA	NIG	NIGER
BUR	BURUNDI	PAR	PARAGUAY
CAM	CAMEROON	RWA	RWANDA
CAR	CENTRAL	SIN	SINGAPORE
	AFRICAN REPUBLIC	SWI	SWITZERLAND
CON	CONGO		

Source: World Bank Atlas 1979

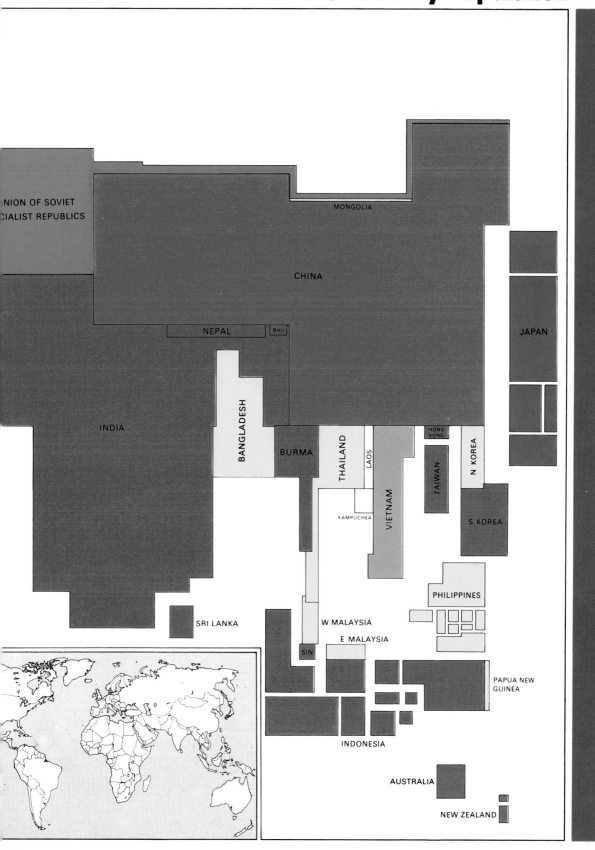

UNION OF SOVIET SOCIALIST REPUBLICS

MONGOLIA

CHINA

JAPAN

NEPAL

BHU

INDIA

BANGLADESH

BURMA

THAILAND

LAOS

HONG KONG

N KOREA

VIETNAM

TAIWAN

KAMPUCHEA

S KOREA

SRI LANKA

W MALAYSIA

PHILIPPINES

E MALAYSIA

SIN

PAPUA NEW GUINEA

INDONESIA

AUSTRALIA

NEW ZEALAND

Antarctica and Its Neighbours

Pacific Ocean

Antarctic Circle

Bellinghausen Sea

Amundsen Sea

Weddell Sea

Ross Sea

+ South Pole

ANTARCTICA

NEW ZEALAND
• Christchurch

Atlantic Ocean

Melbourne •

AUSTRALIA

Indian Ocean

• Cape Town

SOUTH
LESOTHO   AFRICA

NAMIBIA

CHILE   ARGENTINA

Buenos Aires •

URUGUAY

BRAZIL

Territorial Claims:
A Difference of Opinion

Belgium, Japan, South Africa and the USSR do not
formally recognise any claims; the USA and the
USSR 'reserve their rights' and the USA has
rejected all existing claims.

NORWAY

ARGENTINA

BRITAIN

CHILE

AUSTRALIA

FRANCE

AUSTRALIA

NEW ZEALAND

60°

Resources of the
Antarctic seas

Antarctic krill

Antarctic cod

Antarctic icefish

Minke whale

The Lure of Wealth

Antarctica, one hundred million years ago, showing what were until then continuous mountain ranges: the Transantarctic Mountains connected to the Andes in South America; the Central Antarctic Mountains connected to the Rand in South Africa and to mineral rich areas in Australia.

Metallic minerals already located in Antarctica include chromium (Cr), nickel (Ni), cobalt (Co), copper (Cu), gold (Au), silver (Ag), manganese (Mu), molybdenum (Mo), iron (Fe), titanium (Ti), platinum (Pt), lead (Pb), zinc (Zu), tin (Su), uranium (U). There are also vast reserves of coal and deposits of oil and natural gas: for the present, uneconomic to exploit.

major

minor

historically connected mineral resources

located mineral deposits in Antarctica

The settlers

Scientific stations south of the 60th parallel, 1979

US : Canada

US : Canada

GREENLAND

SPITZBERGEN
Norway : USSR

'Cod wars'
Iceland : UK (also W. Germany,
Norway)

Iceland : Norway

ICELAND

FAROE ISLANDS
UK : Denmark

NORWAY

SWEDEN

CANADA

UNITED KINGDOM

DENMARK

see inset

UK : Ireland

IRELAND

NETH.

BEL.

GERMANY

W

FRANCE

POL

CZECH

AUS.

Y

Canada : France

US : Canada

UK : France

inset

ITALY

UNITED STATES OF AMERICA

US : Canada

Spain : EEC

SPAIN

PORTUGAL

Cuba : EEC

Spain : Portugal

BERMUDA

Spain : Morocco

TUNISIA

MOROCCO

ALGERIA

LIB

MEXICO

BAHAMAS

CUBA

MAURITANIA

MALI

NIGER

CH

DOMINICAN REPUBLIC
PUERTO RICO

JAMAICA

BELIZE

HONDURAS

HAITI

CAPE VERDE

SENEGAL

GUATEMALA

US : Colombia : Nicaragua

GAMBIA

EL SALVADOR

Venezuela : Colombia

NICARAGUA

Venezuela : Netherlands Antilles

GUINEA-BISSAU

GUINEA

UPPER
VOLTA

COSTA RICA

VENEZUELA

TRINIDAD AND TOBAGO

Guyana : Venezuela

SIERRA LEONE

IVORY
COAST

GHANA

BENIN

TOGO

NIGERIA

PANAMA

SURINAM

LIBERIA

CAMEROON

C

COLOMBIA

GUYANA

Cameroon : Nigeria
EQUATORIAL GUINEA

ECUADOR

Equatorial Guinea : Gabon

GABON

CONGO

'Tuna wars'
US : Peru

(also Canada, Japan
USSR, Greece)

(also Ecuador,
Nicaragua
Mexico, Costa Rica,
Colombia)

PERU

BRAZIL

ANG

NAM

Bolivia : Peru : Chile

BOLIVIA

CHILE

PARAGUAY

inset

★ Major demarcation disputes 1974-79

Major fishing disputes, 1974-79

Exclusive Economic Zones

Where geographically possible, most littoral
states have claimed an Exclusive Economic
Zone extending 200 nautical miles, or 350
miles or more into the continental shelf. This
map shows how an extension of national
jurisdiction to 200 miles off all coasts,
including those of islands, could affect as
much as one third of the seas that cover
70 per cent of the globe.

URUGUAY

PORTUGAL

ARGENTINA

FRANCE

Italy : Yugoslavia

YUGOSLAVIA

ITALY

Albania : Yugoslavia

ALBANIA

Albania : Greece

GRE

SPAIN

MALTA

Italy : Tunisia

Libya : Tunisia

Chile : Argentina

UK : Argentina

FALKLAND ISLANDS

MOROCCO

ALGERIA

TUNISIA

LIBYA

Source: B. Buzan, A Sea of Troubles? London,
International Institute of Strategic Studies,
1978 and press reports

One year's launching of satellites

Of the 159 satellites launched in 1978, 119 were Soviet (mainly short-lived), 30 American (longer-lived), 4 Japanese, 2 Western European, and one each Chinese, Czechoslovak, Canadian and NATO.

Of the total, probably 112 were military (91 Soviet, 19 American 1 Chinese and 1 NATO), which brought the number of military satellites ever launched to 1603, three-quarters of all artificial satellites. Over half the military satellites are for surveillance, a quarter for military communications and the rest for geodesy, navigation, early warning of attack and meteorology.

1978 saw two more Russian firsts in space: the launching of a primitive hunter-killer satellite in May, and the crash, in the Canadian Northwest, of Kosmos 945, which contaminated a large area with radioactive debris.

Tyuratam

Lop Nor

Tanegashima

Sources: COSPAR Information Bulletin   SIPRI, World Armaments and Disarmaments Yearbook 1979

Foreign military presence, early 1980

- army: major combat force (10,000 or above)
- army: minor combat force (250 and above)
- military advisors, intelligence, communications or surveillance
- air force (bases or landing rights)
- navy (bases or anchorage rights)

Source: A. J. Cottrell and T. H. Moore, US Overseas Bases, 1977
International Institute of Strategic Studies
Press reports

ICELAND

BELGIUM NETHERLANDS SWEDEN
NORWAY

IRELAND DENMARK
UNITED KINGDOM POLAN

WEST EAST
GERMANY CZECH
SWITZ AUSTRIA HUN
FRANCE RO

PORTUGAL SPAIN ITALY YUGO
ALB

GREENLAND

CANADA

UNITED STATES OF AMERICA

MEXICO

GUATEMALA
EL SALVADOR
COSTA RICA

HONDURAS
NICARAGUA
PANAMA

CUBA
JAMAICA

DOMINICAN REPUBLIC

BARBADOS
TRINIDAD AND
TOBAGO

VENEZUELA GUYANA
SURINAM

COLOMBIA

ECUADOR

PERU

BRAZIL

AUSTRIA JORDAN

BOLIVIA

PARAGUAY

BURUNDI LEBANON SWAZILAND

CHILE

URUGUAY

FIJI MALAWI SWITZERLAND

ARGENTINA

ISRAEL RWANDA SYRIA

FALKLAND
ISLANDS

MOROCCO

TUNISIA

ALGERIA

MAURITANIA MALI NIGER

CAPE VERDE
SENEGAL

GUINEA UPPER
VOLTA
SIERRA LEONE GHANA BENIN NIGERIA

LIBERIA IVORY
COAST EQUATORIAL CAMEROON
GUINEA
TOGO GABON
CONGO

ANGO

NAMIE

Proportion of GNP spent on military uses in 1977

over 20%	2.5 - 5%
10.1 - 20%	below 2.5%
5.1 - 10%	data not available

Extreme range: Oman 42.7% - Mauritius 0.2%

**Proportion of central government income
spent on military uses in 1977**
where data available

50% and over

25%

10%

below
5%

Extreme range:
Equatorial Guinea 61.8% - Mauritius 0.5%

Source: USACDA World Military Expenditure and Arms Transfers 1969-77

UNION OF SOVIET SOCIALIST REPUBLICS

MONGOLIA

N KOREA

CHINA

S KOREA

JAPAN

TURKEY

CYPRUS

SYRIA

IRAQ

IRAN

AFGHANISTAN

PAKISTAN

KUWAIT

SAUDI ARABIA

UAE

EGYPT

OMAN

N YEMEN

SOUTH YEMEN

SUDAN

NEPAL

INDIA

BANGLADESH

BURMA

LAOS

TAIWAN

KAM

VIETNAM

THAILAND

PHILIPPINES

SRI LANKA

MALAYSIA

ETHIOPIA

SOMALIA

UGANDA

KENYA

SINGAPORE

INDONESIA

TANZANIA

COMOROS

MADAGASCAR

PAPUA NEW GUINEA

ZIMB

AUSTRALIA

Military Spending by Region

Europe
$232,600m

North America
$105,100m

Middle East
$26,900m

East Asia
$50,400m

South Asia
$4200m

Africa
$6100m

Oceania
$3000m

Latin America
$5900m

NATO countries
$164,700 million

Warsaw Pact countries
$163,000 million

World expenditure on
military uses in 1977
$433,900 million

Nuclear weapons delivery systems
present and planned
early 1980

hundreds   tens

ICBMs (land based
Inter-Continental Ballistic Missiles)

IRBMs
(Intermediate Range Ballistic Missiles)

SLBMs (long-range
Submarine-Launched Ballistic Missiles)

Long-range bombers with air launch
capability

Long-range cruise missiles agreed in
principle end of 1979 (US controlled)

Pershing missiles (US controlled)

Source: Press reports
SIPRI

Full and candidate members of the nuclear club

nuclear weapons states 'which have manufactured
and exploded a nuclear weapon or other nuclear
explosive device'

suspected nuclear weapons states 'widely reputed
to have constructed or to be able to construct
within a very few hours several nuclear weapons'

near nuclear weapons states 'now technically and
industrially able to develop the capability to
manufacture and explode a nuclear weapon or other
nuclear explosive device or will become so by
the year 2000'

states unlikely to be candidates for the nuclear
club before the year 2000

UNION OF SOVIET SOCIALIST REPUBLICS

MONGOLIA

JAPAN

KOREA

TURKEY

CYPRUS
LEBANON
ISRAEL
IRAQ
SYRIA

IRAN

AFGHANISTAN

CHINA

2 ICBMs
in 1979

EGYPT

KUWAIT
BAHRAIN
QATAR
U.A.E.
OMAN

PAKISTAN

NEPAL

B
DESH

TAIWAN

HONG KONG

SAUDI
ARABIA

INDIA

BURMA
LAOS

SUDAN

N
YEMEN
S
YEMEN

PHILIPPINES

ETHIOPIA

SOMALIA

KAM

VIETNAM

KENYA

SRI LANKA

TANZANIA

MALAYSIA
SINGAPORE

W

INDONESIA

PAPUA
NEW GUINEA

MALAWI

MADAGASCAR

MOZAMBIQUE

AUSTRALIA

Kill capacity
Areas of destruction: from the Hiroshima bomb to the ICBM of the mid 1980s

Hiroshima

Hiroshima

Hiroshima

Hiroshima bomb
3 sq. miles

current US ICBMs
50 sq. miles

US ICBMs for mid 1980s
290 sq. miles

NEW ZEALAND

CANADA

UNITED STATES OF AMERICA

MEXICO

BELIZE
GUATEMALA
EL SALVADOR
COSTA RICA

BAHAMAS
CUBA
HAITI   DOMINICAN REPUBLIC
HONDURAS
NICARAGUA

BARBADOS
TRINIDAD AND TOBAGO

VENEZUELA
COLOMBIA
GUYANA
SURINAM
FRENCH GUIANA

ECUADOR

PERU

BRAZIL

BOLIVIA

PARAGUAY

ARGENTINA
CHILE
URUGUAY

W. GERMANY

NETHERLANDS
BELGIUM

UNITED
KINGDOM

IRELAND

NORWAY

SWEDEN

DEN

E
GERMANY

CZECH

POLAND

HU

AUST

FRANCE

YUG

ITALY

ALB

PORT   SPAIN

SWITZERLAND

GREECE

FINL

MOROCCO

TUNISIA

ALGERIA

LIB

MAURITANIA   MALI

CAPE VERDE

SENEGAL

GUINEA-BISSAU
GUINEA
SIERRA LEONE
LIBERIA

IVORY
COAST

UPPER
VOLTA

NIGER

NIGERIA

C

BENIN
TOGO
GHANA

CAMEROON

GABON
CONGO

C

ANG

NAM

© Copyright Pluto Press

UNION OF SOVIET SOCIALIST REPUBLICS

MONGOLIA

TURKEY

IRAQ

IRAN

AFGHANISTAN

PAKISTAN

GYPT

inset

KUWAIT

BAHRAIN

QATAR

U.A.E.

SAUDI ARABIA

OMAN

N YEMEN

S.YEMEN

DJIBOUTI

SUDAN

ETHIOPIA

SOMALIA

NEPAL

B DESH

BURMA

INDIA

SRI LANKA

THAILAND

KAM

LA

VIETNAM

MALAYSIA

SINGAPORE

INDONESIA

PHILIPPINES

CHINA

TAIWAN

N KOREA

S

JAPAN

KOREA

UGANDA

KENYA

TANZANIA

COMOROS

MBIA

MALAWI

MOZAMBIQUE

ZIMBABWE

MADAGASCAR

UTH AFRICA

PAPUA NEW GUINEA

AUSTRALIA

NEW ZEALAND

inset

TURKEY

SYRIA

LEB

ISRAEL

JORDAN

IRAQ

SAUDI ARABIA

Numbers of combat aircraft in 1979
(figures rounded)

100 combat aircraft

under 100 combat aircraft

Extreme range: e.g. Nicaragua 4
— USSR 6079

Source: International Institute for Strategic Studies

CANADA

ICELAND

DENMARK

NETHERLANDS

BELGIUM

LUXEMBOURG

E GERMANY

POLA

UNITED STATES OF AMERICA

UNITED KINGDOM

FRANCE

W. GERMANY

CZECH

SWITZ

AUSTRIA

HUNGAR

ITALY

PORTUGAL

SPAIN

YUGO

ALBANIA

GRE

MEXICO

GUATEMALA

EL SALVADOR

HONDURAS

NICARAGUA

PANAMA

COLOMBIA

VENEZUELA

GUYANA

DOMINICAN REPUBLIC

CUBA

TUNISIA

ECUADOR

PERU

BRAZIL

B

URUGUAY

ARGENTINA

CHILE

MOROCCO

ALGERIA

LIBYA

SENEGAL

G

IC

MAU

G BISSAU

GH

TO

EQUATORIAL GUINEA

GABON

CONGO

A

S A

Imports into Latin America
1973-77 US $3,558 million

Imports into Africa
1973-77 US $7,738 million

Weapons exports and imports

Suppliers of world arms imports 1973-77

Shares of world arms exports/imports depending on whether countries are net exporters or net importers,1973-77

=1.0%

major exporters

=0.1%

Major arms suppliers (50% or more):

12.05% others

6.24%

5.1%

3.1%

37.86%

32.81%

1.79%

1.65%

USA	W. Germany
USSR	Italy
France	China
UK	many suppliers or data not available

World total US $71,320 million

Source: US Arms Control and Disarmament Agency,
World Military Expenditures and Arms Transfers 1968-77, 1979

UNION OF SOVIET SOCIALIST REPUBLICS

Imports into South Asia
1973-77 US $2,417 million

Imports into East Asia
1973-77 US $11,046 million

Imports into Middle East
1973-77 US $23,767 million

CANADA

UNITED STATES OF AMERICA

USA ⬤ N. Vietnam
USA ⬤ Cambodia
USA ⬤ Laos

MEXICO

BAHAMAS

CUBA Cuba ⬤ Angola
HAITI DOMINICAN REPUBLIC
JAMAICA PUERTO RICO

GUATEMALA HONDURAS
EL SALVADOR
El Salvador ⬤ Honduras
NICARAGUA
COSTA RICA BARBADOS
PANAMA TRINIDAD AND TOBAGO

VENEZUELA GUYANA
SURINAM

COLOMBIA

ECUADOR

PERU

BRAZIL

BOLIVIA

PARAGUAY

URUGUAY

CHILE ARGENTINA

ICELAND

NORWAY SWEDEN

DENMARK

IRELAND UNITED KINGDOM

N E
W GERMANY
S B
CZE
AUST
YUG
ITALY

France ⬤ Libya
France ⬤ Morocco

FRANCE

PORTUGAL SPAIN

MOROCCO TUNISIA

Morocco ⬤ Algeria
Morocco ⬤ France ALGERIA LI

MAURITANIA MALI NIGER F

CAPE VERDE

SENEGAL
GAMBIA
GUINEA-BISSAU
GUINEA UPPER
VOLTA
SIERRA LEONE IVORY GHANA BENIN NIGERIA
LIBERIA COAST TOGO
CAMEROON
EQUATORIAL GUINEA
GABON CONG

Angola ⬤ AN
S. Africa ⬤
NAM

Source: Press reports

States at war (professional armies engaged on both sides) at some time during the 1970s

▬ area of conflict

⬤ ⬤ states at war

© Copyright Pluto Press

UNION OF SOVIET SOCIALIST REPUBLICS

USSR ◄► China
USSR ◄► Afghanistan

MONGOLIA

China ◄► USSR

N KOREA
S S. Korea

JAPAN

N. Vietnam

TURKEY

CYPRUS SYRIA
ISRAEL IRAQ

Egypt
GYPT

KUWAIT
BAHRAIN
QATAR
U.A.E.
OMAN

inset 1

IRAN

USSR Afgh.
AFGH.

PAKISTAN

Pakistan ◄► India

NEPAL

BHUTAN

B
DESH BURMA

CHINA

China ◄► USSR
China ◄► Vietnam

TAIWAN

HONG KONG

SAUDI ARABIA

Saudi Arabia
N. Yemen S YEMEN
N YEMEN S. Yemen

INDIA

LAOS VIETNAM

THAILAND

KAMPU-
CHEA

inset 2

PHILIPPINES

SUDAN

ETHIOPIA

Ethiopia Somalia

SOMALIA

SRI LANKA

MALAYSIA

SINGAPORE

W

Jganda KENYA

Tanzania

TANZANIA

COMOROS

INDONESIA

PAPUA
NEW GUINEA

Indonesia ◄► Timor

MBIA
MALAWI
Rhodesia

IMBABWE
hodesia

NA
MOZAMBIQUE

MADAGASCAR

Mozambique

AUSTRALIA

Australia ◄► N. Vietnam

inset 2

CHINA

Vietnam ◄► China

H
7

ca ◄► Angola

LAOS

N. Vietnam
S. Vietnam
USA
Australia
S. Korea

inset 1

Turkey ◄► Cyprus

TURKEY

THAILAND

Laos ◄► S. Vietnam
USA

Cyprus Turkey

SYRIA

Israel Leb
Syria

IRAQ

Israel
ISRAEL

Israel Jordan

Egypt Israel

SAUDI
ARABIA

KAMPUCHEA

Cambodia ◄► Vietnam
USA

Cambodia ◄► S. Vietnam

NEW ZEALAND

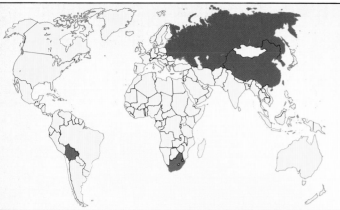

Antimony
World production 1976:
69,700 metric tons

Countries with 5 per cent
of more of world
production 1976:

Bolivia   21.9 per cent
China   17.2 per cent
South Africa 16.48 per cent
USSR   11 per cent

Total produced by
top four countries:
66.58 per cent

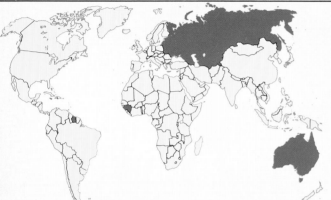

Bauxite
World production 1976:
73,800 thousand metric
tons

Countries with 5 per cent
or more of world
production 1976:

Australia 26.69 per cent
Guinea   13.9 per cent
Jamaica   14.19 per cent
Surinam   6.2 per cent
USSR   6.2 per cent

Total produced by
top five countries:
67.28 per cent

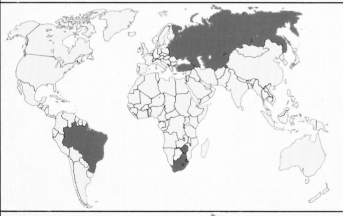

Chrome
World production 1976:
4030 thousand metric tons

Countries with 5 per cent
or more of world
production 1976:

Albania   8.4 per cent
Brazil   8.3 per cent
South Africa 26.97 per cent
Turkey   8.7 per cent
USSR   21.8 per cent
Zimbabwe   7.56 per cent

Total produced by
top six countries:
81.73 per cent

Copper
World production 1976:
8000 thousand metric tons

Countries with 5 per cent
or more of world
production 1976:

Canada   9.13 per cent
Chile   12.66 per cent
USSR   14.1 per cent
USA   18.2 per cent
Zaire   5.54 per cent
Zambia   10.62 per cent

Total produced by
top six countries:
70.25 per cent

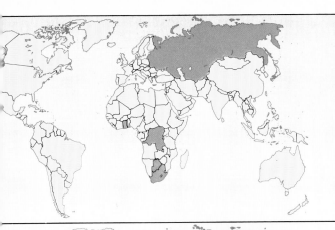

Diamonds
(Gems and industrial diamonds combined)
World production 1976:
38,100 thousand metric carats

Countries with 5 per cent
or more of world production 1976:

Botswana   6.19 per cent
Ghana   5.99 per cent
South Africa 18.43 per cent
USSR   25.98 per cent
Zaire   31 per cent

South Africa is by far the biggest
producer of gem stones

Total produced by
top five countries:
87.59 per cent

Iron Ore
World production 1976:
263,799 thousand metric
tons
Countries with 5 per cent
or more of world
production 1976:

Liberia   5.3 per cent
Sweden   7.2 per cent
USSR   49.6 per cent
USA   19 per cent

Total produced by
top four countries:
81.1 per cent

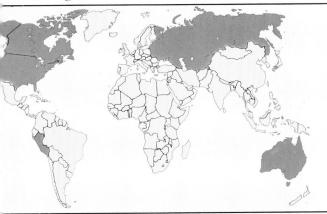

Lead
World production 1976:
3330 thousand metric tons
Countries with 5 per cent
or more of world
production 1976:

Australia 11.9 per cent
Canada   7.69 per cent
Peru   5.49 per cent
USSR   14.1 per cent
USA   16.6 per cent

Total produced by
top five countries:
55.78 per cent

Manganese
World production 1976:
9840 thousand metric tons
Countries with 5 per cent
or more of world
production 1976:

Australia   7.7 per cent
Brazil   12.88 per cent
Gabon   11.11 per cent
India   6.76 per cent
South Africa 24.48 per cent
USSR   30.4 per cent

Total produced by
top six countries:
93.4 per cent

Source: *UN Statistical Yearbook 1978*

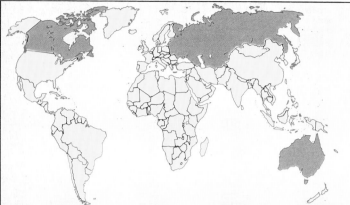

Nickel

World production 1976:
803,900 metric tons

Countries with 5 per cent
or more of world
production 1976:

Australia	10 per cent
Canada	29.5 per cent
New Caledonia	
(Fr colony)	14.79 per cent
USSR	19.9 per cent

Total produced by
top four countries:
74.64 per cent

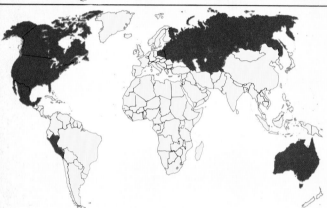

Silver

World production 1976:
9690 metric tons
Countries with 5 per cent
or more of world
production 1976:

Australia	7.45 per cent
Canada	13.2 per cent
Mexico	13.68 per cent
Peru	12.13 per cent
Poland	5.15 per cent
USSR	14.13 per cent
USA	11 per cent

Total produced by
top seven countries:
76.7 per cent

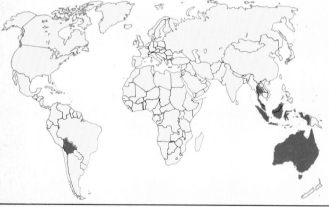

Tin

World production 1976:
179,800 metric tons
Countries with 5 per cent
or more of world
production 1976:

Australia	5.78 per cent
Bolivia	16.86 per cent
Indonesia	13 per cent
Malaysia	35.26 per cent
Thailand	11.37 per cent

Total produced by
top five countries:
82.27 per cent

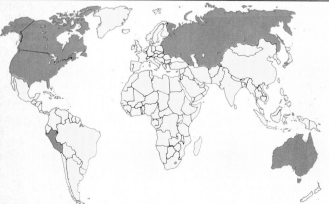

Zinc

World production 1976:
5520 thousand metric tons
Countries with 5 per cent
or more of world
production 1976:

Australia	8.68 per cent
Canada	17.79 per cent
Peru	8.27 per cent
USSR	13 per cent
USA	7.96 per cent

Total produced by
top five countries:
55.7 per cent

14. The World Mineral Powers

The World Mineral Powers

All countries with 5 per
cent or more of at least four
major minerals, 1976

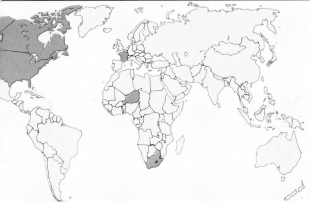

Uranium
World production 1976
(excluding USSR, Eastern
Europe, China)
22,293 metric tons
Countries with 5 per cent
or more of world
production 1976:

Canada	21.75 per cent
France	9.25 per cent
Niger	6.54 per cent
South Africa	15.3 per cent
USA	43.95 per cent

Total produced by
top five countries:
96.79 per cent

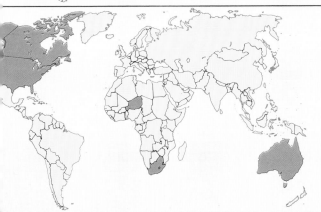

Uranium reserves
January 1978

World reserves at a market
price of less than US$30 a lb.
(excluding USSR, Eastern
Europe, China): 1650 thousand
metric tons

Countries with 5 per cent
or more of world reserves:

Australia	17.5 per cent
Canada	10.12 per cent
Niger	9.69 per cent
South Africa	18.54 per cent
USA	31.69 per cent

Total produced by top five
countries: 87.54 per cent

Source: *UN Statistical Yearbook 1978*

GREENLAND

ICELAND

NORWAY SWEDEN

DENMARK

IRELAND UNITED
KINGDOM N W E
B GERMANY
CZECH
FRANCE AUST
SW

ITALY

PORTUGAL SPAIN

TUNISIA

MOROCCO ALGERIA L

CANADA

MAURITANIA
MALI NIGER

SENEGAL
GAMBIA
GUINEA UPPER
VOLTA
SIERRA LEONE IVORY NIGERIA
COAST GHANA BENIN CAMEROON
TOGO
LIBERIA

EQUATORIAL GUINEA
GABON
CONGO

ANC

NAM

UNITED STATES OF AMERICA

MEXICO

BAHAMAS

CUBA
JAMAICA DOMINICAN REPUBLIC
HAITI PUERTO RICO
HONDURAS
GUATEMALA
EL SALVADOR
NICARAGUA

COSTA RICA
PANAMA

BARBADOS
TRINIDAD AND TOBAGO

VENEZUELA
GUYANA
SURINAM

COLOMBIA

ECUADOR

PERU

BRAZIL

BOLIVIA

PARAGUAY

CHILE

URUGUAY

ARGENTINA

World energy consumption, 1978

Hydro   Nuclear **2.3%**
6%

Coal
27.1%

46%   Oil

18.6%

Natural gas

Source: BP Statistical Review of the World Oil Industry 1978

Domestic production and consumption of all recorded forms of energy in 1976

Countries with an energy surplus:

Production more than 10 times greater than consumption

Production greater than consumption but less than 10 times greater

Countries with an energy deficit:

Consumption greater than production but less than 10 times greater

Consumption more than 10 times greater than production

data not available

Data based on millions metric tons coal equivalent

Source: UN Statistical Yearbook 1978

UNION OF SOVIET SOCIALIST REPUBLICS

TURKEY

YPRUS
LEBANON
ISRAEL
JO

IRAQ

SYRIA

IRAN

AFGHANISTAN

MONGOLIA

CHINA

N KOREA
S KOREA
JAPAN

TAIWAN

HONG KONG

KUWAIT

QATAR
UNITED ARAB EMIRATES

GYPT

SAUDI ARABIA

OMAN

N
YEMEN

S
YEMEN

PAKISTAN

NEPAL

BHUTAN

B
DESH

INDIA

BURMA

LAOS

THAILAND

KAM

VIETNAM

PHILIPPINES

SUDAN

DJIBOUTI

ETHIOPIA

SOMALIA

BAHRAIN

MAURITIUS

SRI LANKA

BRUNEI

MALAYSIA

KENYA

NDA

UNDI

TANZANIA

MADAGASCAR

BIA

MBABWE

MOZAMBIQUE

TH
CA

S

INDONESIA

PAPUA
NEW
GUINEA

AUSTRALIA

Coal production and consumption in 1978
Countries with annual production more
than 10 million metric tons
Source: UN World Energy Supplies 1973-78

UNITED KINGDOM

EAST GERMANY

BELGIUM

POLAND

CZECHOSLOVAKIA

HUNGARY

WEST
GERMANY

ITALY

ROMANIA

USSR

BULGARIA

N KOREA

S KOREA

CANADA

FRANCE

YUGOSLAVIA

JAPAN

INDIA

UNITED STATES OF AMERICA

SOUTH AFRICA

CHINA

AUSTRALIA

NEW ZEALAND

Coal Power

Scale

☐ consumption: 10 million metric tons

■ production: 10 million metric tons

The Big Producers and the Big Consumers

consumption/production to constant scale

CANADA

UNITED
STATES OF AMERICA

MEXICO

BAHAMAS

CUBA

HAITI DOMINICAN REPUBLIC
PUERTO RICO
JAMAICA

GUATEMALA HONDURAS
EL SALVADOR
NICARAGUA

COSTA RICA PANAMA

GRENADA
BARBADOS
TRINIDAD AND TOBAGO

VENEZUELA
GUYANA
SURINAM

COLOMBIA

ECUADOR

PERU

BRAZIL

BOLIVIA

PARAGUAY

URUGUAY

ARGENTINA

CHILE

NORWAY

FINL

SWEDEN

UNITED
KINGDOM

IRELAND

DENMARK

NETH

BEL

POLAND

CZECHOSLOVAKIA

AUSTRIA

HUNGARY

FRANCE

YUGOSLA

PORTUGAL SPAIN

ITALY

ALBANI

SWITZERLAND

TUNISIA

MOROCCO

ALGERIA

LIB

MAURITANIA

MALI

NIGER

C

SENEGAL

GAMBIA

UPPER
VOLTA

GUINEA

NIGERIA

SIERRA LEONE

IVORY
COAST

GHANA

BENIN

TOGO

LIBERIA

EQUATORIAL GUINEA

CAMEROON

C

GABON

CONGO

ANG

NAMI

**Nuclear power's share of installed
electricity generating capacity in 1978**

- over 15%
- 12.1 — 15%
- 9.1 — 12%
- 6.1 — 9%
- 3.1 — 6%
- 3% and below
- no nuclear power capacity in 1978

**nuclear power reactors above
20 mega-watts (E) in 1978**

- ten reactors
- one reactor

**nuclear power reactors
planned for 1984**

- ten reactors
- one reactor

5.85%

94.15%

Nuclear power's share of
world electricity generating
capacity 1978 5.85%

Source: SIPRI, World Armaments and Disarmament 1979
UN, World Energy Supplies 1973-78, New York 1979

GREENLAND ICELAND DENMARK

CANADA

UNITED STATES OF AMERICA

WEST GERMANY

NETHERLANDS

BAHAMAS

MEXICO

CUBA HAITI DOM REP

IRELAND

JAMAICA

UNITED KINGDOM

GUATEMALA MARTINIQUE

BELIZE GUADALOUPE

HONDURAS BELGIUM

EL SALVADOR LUXEMBOURG

NICARAGUA BARBADOS

COSTA RICA

NETHERLANDS ANTILLES

F

PANAMA TRINIDAD AND TOBAGO

VENEZUELA GUYANA

COLOMBIA

ECUADOR SPAIN

PERU

BRAZIL PORTUGAL

B

PARA

URUGUAY

CHILE ARGENTINA

Surplus and Deficit Regions

food surplus
food deficit

States with a food trade surplus

■ More than $1 billion

□ Less than $1 billion

States with a food trade deficit

■ More than $1 billion

□ Less than $1 billion

Shares of world exports or imports of world food trade, 1977 depending on whether states have a food surplus or food deficit

1.0%

0.1%

Source: FAO Trade Yearbook 1977

CANADA

UNITED STATES
OF AMERICA

MEXICO

BAHAMAS

CUBA

JAMAICA
HAITI
DOMINICAN REPUBLIC
PUERTO RICO

GUATEMALA
HONDURAS
EL SALVADOR
NICARAGUA

BARBADOS

COSTA RICA
TRINIDAD AND TOBAGO
PANAMA

VENEZUELA
GUYANA
SURINAM

COLOMBIA

ECUADOR

PERU

BRAZIL

BOLIVIA

PARAGUAY

URUGUAY

CHILE
ARGENTINA

ICELAND

WEST
GERMANY

NORWAY

SWEDEN

IRELAND

DENMARK

UNITED
KINGDOM

NETHERLANDS

GERMANY
W   E

BEL

POLAND

CZECH

SWITZ   AUSTRIA
HUNGARY

PORTUGAL

FRANCE

YUGOSLAV

SPAIN

ITALY

ALBANIA

TUNISIA

MOROCCO

ALGERIA

LI

MAURITANIA

MALI

NIGER

SENEGAL

GAMBIA

GUINEA

UPPER
VOLTA

SIERRA LEONE

LIBERIA
IVORY
COAST

GHANA

TOGO

BENIN

NIGERIA

CAMEROON

EQUATORIAL
GUINEA

GABON

CONGO

AN

NAM

LUXEMBOURG
MALAWI
RWANDA
SINGAPORE
SWAZILAND

**Manufacturing output
by value (US $millions) in the mid 1970s**
Where data available

each $100,000 million
figures rounded

$50,001 — under $100,000 million

$10,001 – $50,000 million

$5000 — $10,000 million

under $5000 million

Source: UN Yearbooks of Industrial Statistics, 1975, 1976, 1977

© *Copyright Pluto Press*

UNION OF SOVIET SOCIALIST REPUBLICS

MONGOLIA

CHINA

JAPAN

N K

S KOREA

TURKEY

CYPRUS

LEBANON SYRIA

EL

IRAQ

JORDAN

IRAN

AFGHANISTAN

KUWAIT

PAKISTAN

QATAR

GYPT

SAUDI

ARABIA

UAE

OMAN

NEPAL

TAIWAN

BURMA

INDIA

BANGLADESH

VIETNAM

HONG KONG

LAOS

N

YEMEN

S YEMEN

THAILAND

KAM

PHILIPPINES

UDAN

SRI LANKA

ETHIOPIA

SOMALIA

UGANDA

KENYA

MALAYSIA

SINGAPORE

TANZANIA

INDONESIA

PAPUA

NEW GUINEA

MOZAMBIQUE

MBABWE

S

MADAGASCAR

AUSTRALIA

The Power of Persuasion

Advertising expenditure
as a proportion of the value of industrial output in 1970
Where data available

| | over 6% | | 4.1 – 6% | | 2 – 4% | | below 2% |

Source: UNCTAD, The Role of Trade Marks in Developing Countries, 1979.

NEW ZEALAND

CANADA

UNITED STATES OF AMERICA

MEXICO

BAHAMAS

CUBA

BELIZE
GUATEMALA HONDURAS
EL SALVADOR
NICARAGUA

JAMAICA HAITI DOMINICAN REPUBLIC
PUERTO RICO

BARBADOS
TRINIDAD AND TOBAGO

COSTA RICA
PANAMA

VENEZUELA GUYANA
SURINAM

COLOMBIA

ECUADOR

PERU

BRAZIL

BOLIVIA

PARAGUAY

CHILE

ARGENTINA

URUGUAY

NORWAY SWEDEN FINLAND

IRELAND
UNITED
KINGDOM

DENMARK

NETHER-
LANDS
BELG-
IUM
WEST
GERMANY

EAST
GERMANY

POLAND

CZECHOSLOVAKIA

PORTUGAL

SPAIN

FRANCE

SWITZ

AUSTRIA HUNGARY

YUGOSLAVIA

ITALY

ALBANIA

TUNISIA

MOROCCO

ALGERIA

LI

MAURITANIA

MALI

NIGER

SENEGAL
GAMBIA
GUINEA-BISSAU
GUINEA
SIERRA LEONE
LIBERIA

UPPER
VOLTA

IVORY
COAST
GHANA
TOGO
BENIN

NIGERIA

C

CAMEROON

EQUATORIAL
GUINEA
GABON
CONGO

AN

NAM

BERMUDA

CAYMAN ISLANDS

ICELAND

MALTA

MAURITIUS

SEYCHELLES

SINGAPORE

WESTERN SAMOA

Scientists and engineers per 100,000 population in mid 1970s

over 200

151 — 200

101 — 150

51 — 100

11 — 50

10 and below

data not available

Extreme range: USSR 488 — Honduras 0.17

Source: UNESCO Statistical Yearbook 1977
UN Demographic Yearbooks 1976, 1977

UNION OF SOVIET SOCIALIST REPUBLICS

MONGOLIA

TURKEY

CYPRUS SYRIA

ISRAEL IRAQ IRAN AFGHANISTAN

KUWAIT PAKISTAN NEPAL

QATAR

U.A.E. OMAN

SAUDI ARABIA

N YEMEN S YEMEN

SUDAN

ETHIOPIA

SOMALIA

UGANDA

KENYA

TANZANIA

MALAWI

MOZAMBIQUE

MADAGASCAR

CHINA

N KOREA S

JAPAN

INDIA

B-DESH

BURMA

TAIWAN

HONG KONG

LAOS

THAILAND

KAM

VIETNAM

PHILIPPINES

SRI LANKA

MALAYSIA

BRUNEI

INDONESIA

PAPUA NEW GUINEA

AUSTRALIA

Brain Drain

CANADA

UNITED KINGDOM

'aid' $2.3b

skilled labour $11.5b

skilled labour $5.5b

UNITED STATES OF AMERICA

'aid' $39.6b

skilled labour $33.9b

'aid' $4.4b

Estimated capital value of skilled immigrant labour
compared with 'development aid'
three examples, 1961-72 in US$ billions

NEW ZEALAND

Source: OECD

GREENLAND

ICELAND
fish 65% of $0.3b

FAROE ISLANDS

NORWAY SWE

DENMARK

IRELAND UNITED
KINGDOM N GERMANY P
CZECH
W E
FRANCE AUST
ITALY

SPAIN

PORTUGAL

CANADA

UNITED STATES OF AMERICA

MEXICO

sugar and honey
88% of $3.7b

CUBA

JAMAICA HAITI

GUATEMALA BELIZE PUERTO RICO
HONDURAS
EL SALVADOR
NICARAGUA
COSTA RICA
PANAMA

BAHAMAS
petroleum
56% of $2.5b

DOMINICAN
REPUBLIC
sugar and honey
63% of $0.9b

BARBADOS
sugar and honey
60% of $0.1b

TRINIDAD
AND TOBAGO
petroleum
50% of $1.8b

VENEZUELA

GUYANA

SURI
NAM

sugar and honey
50% of $0.4b

MOROCCO
crude fertilisers 55% of $1.5b

TUNISIA

ALGERIA

petroleum
85% of $4.3b

LIE

pet
95%

GAMBIA
oil seeds and nuts 57% of $0.05b

MAURITANIA
iron ore,
concentrates
54% of $0.2b

CAPE VERDE

SENEGAL

GUINEA-BISSAU
oil seeds and nuts
80% of $0.006b

SIERRA LEONE
precious stones
60% of $0.04b

LIBERIA
iron ore, concentrates
75% of $0.4b

GUINEA

MALI

UPPER
VOLTA

IVORY
COAST

GHANA
cocoa
76% of $0.76b

GHANA

NIGER
non-ferrous
ores 61% of $0.09b

C
c
62
$(

petroleum
93% of $8.0b
NIGERIA

CAMEROON

GABON
petroleum
83% of $0.9b

TOGO
crude fertilizers
65% of $0.1b

petroleum
73% of $0.2b

CONGO

AN(

ECUADOR
petroleum 58% of $0.9b

COLOMBIA

PERU

BRAZIL

BOLIVIA

PARAGUAY

CHILE
copper ore 54% of $1.7b

URUGUAY

ARGENTINA

FALKLAND ISLANDS

FIJI

HONG KONG

RWANDA

SINGAPORE

sugar and honey
89% of $0.1b

coffee 62% of $0.04b

Sources of export income

More than half of all export income in 1975 came from:

	one product
	two products
	three products
	four products

More than half of all export income in 1975 came from:

| | fifteen products |

Less than half of all export income in 1975 came from:

| | fifteen products |
| | data not available |

DEPENDENCE — DIVERSITY

NAM

One product countries:
Share of total export income (in US$)
from major product is shaded

Source: UNCTAD Handbook of International Trade and Development Statistics 1979

UNION OF SOVIET SOCIALIST REPUBLICS

MONGOLIA

N KOREA

S

JAPAN

CHINA

TURKEY

CYPRUS

SYRIA

IRAQ

IRAN
petroleum
91% of $19.2b

AFGHANISTAN

PAKISTAN

NEPAL

BHUTAN

EGYPT

SAUDI ARABIA
petroleum
93% of $29.7b

inset

OMAN
petroleum 100% of $1.4b

INDIA

B-
DESH

BURMA

TAIWAN

HONG KONG

PHILIPPINES

KIRIBATI
(GILBERT ISLANDS)

SUDAN

DJIBOUTI

S YEMEN
petroleum
and products
74% of $0.1b

N YEMEN
cotton 54%
of $0.16b

ETHIOPIA

animals 69% of $0.09b
SOMALIA

SRI LANKA

LA

KAM

THAILAND

VIETNAM

PAPUA
NEW GUINEA
non-ferrous ores
56% of $0.1b

KENYA

UGANDA
coffee 76% of $0.3b

BRUNEI

MALAYSIA

SINGAPORE

er
of
b

IRE

TANZANIA

BURUNDI
coffee 88% of $0.03b

INDONESIA
petroleum 69% of $7.1b

COMOROS

MOZAMBIQUE

BIA

MALAWI

MAURITIUS
sugar and honey 86% of $0.3b

ZIMBABWE

MADAGASCAR

copper
90% of $0.8b

S

H.AFRICA

AUSTRALIA

inset

petroleum
69% of $0.9b

IRAQ

IRAN

LEBANON

SYRIA

ISRAEL

petroleum 99% of $8.4b

JORDAN

KUWAIT

UNITED
ARAB
EMIRATES
petroleum
98% of $6.7b

petroleum 81% of $9.2b

BAHRAIN
petroleum 74% of $1.1b

QATAR
petroleum 97% of $1.8b

SAUDI

ARABIA

NEW ZEALAND

GREENLAND

ICELAND

CANADA

NETHERLANDS

UNITED STATES OF AMERICA

UNITED
KINGDOM

BELGIUM
AND
LUXEMBOURG

IRELAND

BAHAMAS

MEXICO

CUBA

DOMINICAN REPUBLIC

HONDURAS

HAITI

JAMAICA

FRANCE

GUATEMALA

NICARAGUA

EL SALVADOR

TRINIDAD AND TOBAGO

COSTA
RICA

PANAMA

COLOM

GUYANA

VENEZUELA

SURINAM

ECUADOR

BRAZIL

PORTUGAL

SPAIN

PERU

BO PA

URUGUAY

ARGENTINA

CHILE

Rate of growth or decline in export trade 1969-78

over 100% growth

5.1 - 25% decline

50.1 - 100% growth

25.1 - 50% decline

25.1 - 50% growth

over 50% decline

5.1 - 25% growth

data not available

5% decline - 5% growth

States' shares of total
world exports

= 1%

= 0.1%

Extreme range: S. Yemen 755% growth - Kampuchea 97% decline

World export trade including freight and insurance costs
1969: US$ 246,001 million   1978: US$ 1,190,400 million

Source: IMF Direction of Trade Yearbooks, 1969-75, 1979

GREENLAND
ICELAND

CANADA

UNITED STATES OF AMERICA

DENMARK

NETHERLANDS

BELGIUM
LUXEMBOURG

IRELAND   UNITED
KINGDOM

WEST
GERMANY

FRANCE

ITALY

SPAIN

PORTUGAL

BAHAMAS

DOMINICAN
REPUBLIC

CUBA

HAITI   PUERTO
RICO

JAMAICA

MOROCCO
ALGERIA
TUNISIA

LIBYA   EGYPT

MEXICO

BARBADOS

MAURITANIA M NIGER CHAD SUDAN

GUINEA

VOLTA

GAMBIA

NIGERIA

DJIBOUTI
SOMALIA

CAE

GUATEMALA

EL SALVADOR   HONDURAS
NICARAGUA

TRINIDAD AND TOBAGO

COSTA RICA

PANAMA

COLOMBIA

ECUADOR

PERU

VENEZUELA

GUYANA
SURINAM

F GUYANA

BRAZIL

SENEGAL
SIERRA LEONE
LIBERIA

IVORY COAST

GHANA
TOGO
BENIN

GABON

C
CA
ZAI

UG

T B

KENYA

TANZANIA

ZAMBIA
MALAWI
MOZAMBIQUE

ZI

ANGOLA

NAMIBIA

SOUTH
AFRICA

MADAGASCAR
MAURITIUS
REUNION

SWAZILAND
LESOTHO

MAL

B P UR

CHILE

ARGENTINA

**GNP per head in 1977
in US$**

above $5000

$3001 - $5000

$1001 - $3000

$501 - $1000

$201 - $500

$200 and below

data not available

Extreme range:
UAE $14800 - Bangladesh $80

Source: World Bank Atlas 1979

**Growth/decline in GNPs per head
1970-77**

over 5% growth

3.1 - 5% growth

1.1 - 3% growth

1% growth - 1% decline

1.1 - 3% decline

over 3% decline

data not available

States' shares of total
world GNP in 1977

= 1%

= 0·1%

Extreme range: Macao 17.1% growth - Bahamas 7.2% decline

○ CAPE VERDE
○ COMOROS
◐ GRENADA
● SAO TOME
○ SEYCHELLES

Source: World Bank Atlas 1979

○ BAHRAIN
○ BARBADOS
◑ CAPE VERDE
○ COMOROS
○ FIJI
◐ F POLYNESIA
○ GRENADA
◐ HONG KONG
◑ LUXEMBOURG
○ MACAO
○ MALDIVES
○ MALTA
◑ NEW CALEDONIA
◑ QATAR

○ SAO TOME
○ SEYCHELLES
● SINGAPORE

© *Copyright Pluto Press*

People and Purses

GREENLAND

CANADA

UNITED STATES OF AMERICA

ICELAND

NORWAY   SWED

DENMARK

IRELAND UNITED
         KINGDOM   N
                   B GERMANY CZE

FRANCE   AUST

S   ITALY   YUGO

PORTUGAL SPAIN

MEXICO

BAHAMAS

CUBA

HAITI DOMINICAN REPUBLIC

BELIZE
GUATEMALA   JAMAICA
EL SALVADOR HONDURAS
         NICARAGUA

COSTA RICA PANAMA
              TRINIDAD AND TOBAGO

VENEZUELA   GUYANA
          SURI
          NAM   FRENCH GUIANA
COLOMBIA

ECUADOR

PERU

BRAZIL

BOLIVIA

PARAGUAY

ARGENTINA
              URUGUAY
CHILE

MOROCCO

ALGERIA   L

MAURITANIA   MALI   NIGER

GAMBIA   SENEGAL
GUINEA-BISSAU   VOLTA
    GUINEA
SIERRA LEONE   IVORY   NIGERIA
LIBERIA   COAST GHANA BENIN

                            CAMEROON
                            GABON
                                 CONGO
TOGO

ANG

NAM

External public debt compared with GNPs at the end of 1977

■ over 80%	20.1 — 40%
60.1 — 80%	20% and below
40.1 — 60%	data not available

Extreme range: Mauritania 111.56% — Nigeria 2.19%

Source: World Bank Atlas and Annual Report 1979 UN, World Statistics in Brief, 1978

Growth/decline in external public debt compared with GNPs between 1970 and 1977

over 200% growth   0-25% decline

101-200% growth   over 25% decline

51 — 100% growth   *where data available*

50% and below growth

Extreme range: Rwanda 1559% growth — Nigeria 68.7% decline

Source: World Bank Atlas 1979 World Bank Annual Reports 1972, 1979

UNION OF SOVIET SOCIALIST REPUBLICS

MONGOLIA

CHINA

TURKEY

IRAQ

IRAN

AFGHANISTAN

PAKISTAN

NEPAL

N KOREA

S

JAPAN

TAIWAN

EGYPT

SAUDI ARABIA

U A E

OMAN

N YEMEN

S YEMEN

DJIBOUTI

SUDAN

ETHIOPIA

SOMALIA

UGANDA

KENYA

B

TANZANIA

COMOROS

INDIA

BDESH

BURMA

VIETNAM

THAILAND

KAM

SRI LANKA

MALAYSIA

SINGAPORE

PHILIPPINES

INDONESIA

PAPUA NEW GUINEA

MALAWI

MADAGASCAR

MBABWE

MOZAMBIQUE

SWAZILAND

LESOTHO

The First Bite

Payments on external debt as a proportion of export income in 1977

over 10%	2.51 — 5%
7.51 — 10%	2.5% and below
5.1 — 7.5%	data not available

Extreme range:
Mexico 48.1%
S. Yemen 0.1%

Source: World Bank Annual Report 1979

Reserves of gold and foreign currency

No. of months of normal imports which could be covered by official reserves (gold and foreign currency) in 1976 or 1977

- one month or less
- 1.1 — 2 months
- 2.1 — 3 months
- 3.1 — 6 months
- 6.1 — 9 months
- 9.1 — 12 months
- over 12 months
- data not available

Extreme range: Bahamas 0.16 of a month or about 5 days — Saudi Arabia 24.6 months

Source: UN Statistical Yearbook 1978

MALTA

MAURITIUS

UNION OF SOVIET SOCIALIST REPUBLICS

MONGOLIA

CHINA

TURKEY

CYPRUS
LEBANON
SYRIA
ISRAEL
JORDAN
IRAQ
KUWAIT
BAHRAIN
QATAR
U.A.E.
OMAN

IRAN

AFGHANISTAN

PAKISTAN

NEPAL

BHUTAN

EGYPT

SAUDI ARABIA

N
YEMEN
S YEMEN

DJIBOUTI

INDIA

B
DESH

BURMA

MACAO
HONG KONG

TAIWAN

N
KOREA
S

JAPAN

SUDAN

ETHIOPIA

SOMALIA

THAILAND
LAOS
KAM
VIETNAM

PHILIPPINES

KENYA

SRI LANKA

BRUNEI

MALAYSIA
SINGAPORE

INDONESIA

PAPUA
NEW GUINEA

UGANDA

TANZANIA

MALAWI

MBIA

BWE

MOZAMBIQUE

MADAGASCAR

H
S

AUSTRALIA

NEW ZEALAND

Imports

Imports per head 1977 US$

above $5000	$201 — $500
$3001 — $5000	$200 and below
$1001 — $3000	data not available
$501 — $1000	

Extreme range: United Arab
Emirates $5989.3 — Burma $9.8

Source: World Bank Atlas 1979   UN Statistical Yearbook 1978

ICELAND

CANADA

IRELAND

UNITED
KINGDOM

NETHERLANDS

BELGIUM

L

UNITED STATES OF AMERICA

FRANCE

MEXICO

TRINIDAD AND TOBAGO

JAMAICA

PORTUGAL

SPAIN

GUATEMALA
EL SALVADOR

HONDURAS
NICARAGUA

COSTA RICA

GUYANA

DOMINICAN
REPUBLIC

PANAMA

PUERTO
RICO

COLOMBIA

VENEZUELA

BARBADOS

ECUADOR

SURINAM

PERU

BRAZIL

B

CHILE

ARGENTINA

URUGUAY

**Government shares of
gross domestic product**

over 25%

20 - 25%

15 - 19%

States' shares of total
world government
income

10 - 14%

= 1%

below 10%

data not
available

= 0·1%

Source : *UN Yearbook of National Accounts Statistics 1977*
US Congress Joint Economic Committee, East European
Economies Post-Helsinki 1977 and Soviet Economy in
a New Perspective 1976

NORWAY

SWEDEN

FINLAND

GERMANY WEST

GERMANY EAST

POLAND

CZECHOSLOVAKIA

UNION OF SOVIET SOCIALIST REPUBLICS

SWITZ

AUSTRIA

HUN

ITALY

GREECE

TURKEY

IRAN

PAKISTAN

INDIA

BANGLADESH

THAILAND

HONG KONG

S KOREA

CYPRUS

SYRIA

KAMPUCHEA

MALAYSIA

PHILIPPINES

LEB

JOR

IRAQ

KUWAIT

SRI LANKA

SIN

ISRAEL

INDONESIA

JAPAN

TUNISIA

SAUDI ARABIA

PAPUA NEW GUINEA

FIJI

MOROCCO

ALGERIA

LIBYA

EGYPT

OMAN

SEN

IC

S YEMEN

SL

AUSTRALIA

GHANA

TOGO

BENIN

NIGERIA

SUD

CAM

GAI

ZAIRE

KEN

ETHIOPIA

ZAM

TANZANIA

MAURITIUS

ZIMB

B

SOUTH AFRICA

MADAGASCAR

NEW ZEALAND

CANADA

UNITED STATES OF AMERICA

MEXICO

BAHAMAS

CUBA

HAITI DOMINICAN REPUBLIC
JAMAICA PUERTO RICO

GUATEMALA HONDURAS
EL SALVADOR
NICARAGUA

COSTA RICA
PANAMA

GRENADA BARBADOS
TRINIDAD AND TOBAGO

VENEZUELA GUYANA
SURINAM

COLOMBIA

ECUADOR

PERU

BRAZIL

BOLIVIA

PARAGUAY

CHILE

URUGUAY

ARGENTINA

NORWAY SWEDEN FIN

DENMARK

IRELAND

UNITED KINGDOM

N GERMANY POLAND

B W E

LUX CZECHOSLOVAK

FRANCE AUSTRIA HUNGARY

SWITZ

YUGOSLAV

ITALY

PORTUGAL SPAIN ALBANIA

TUNISIA

MOROCCO ALGERIA LI

MAURITANIA MALI NIGER

SENEGAL

GAMBIA UPPER VOLTA

GUINEA-BISSAU

GUINEA BENIN NIGERIA

SIERRA LEONE IVORY COAST GHANA

LIBERIA TOGO

CAMEROON

EQUATORIAL GUINEA

GABON

CONGO

AN

NAM

Internal security forces
per 100,000 population
early 1970s

	50 and below
	51 — 100
	101 — 200
	201 — 300
	301 — 500
	over 500
	data not available

includes some people's militia
home guard or equivalent

Source: Robert C. Sellars ed. Armed Forces of the World:
Reference Handbook, 4th ed., New York 1977
ILO Yearbook of Labour Statistics 1977

© Copyright Pluto Press

UNION OF SOVIET SOCIALIST REPUBLICS

MONGOLIA

TURKEY

CYPRUS SYRIA
LEBANON
ISRAEL
IRAQ

IRAN

AFGHANISTAN

PAKISTAN

KUWAIT
BAHRAIN
QATAR
U.A.E

SAUDI
ARABIA

OMAN

N
YEMEN S. YEMEN

GYPT

UDAN

ETHIOPIA

SOMALIA

UGANDA

KENYA

TANZANIA

MALAWI

MOZAMBIQUE

ZIMBABWE

CHINA

N
KOREA
S

JAPAN

NEPAL

BHUTAN

B
DESH

INDIA

BURMA

TAIWAN

HONG KONG

LAOS

THAILAND

KAM

VIETNAM

PHILIPPINES

SRI LANKA

MALAYSIA
SINGAPORE

INDONESIA

PAPUA
NEW GUINEA

AUSTRALIA

NEW ZEALAND

Workers in public administration (excluding
teachers and soldiers) as a proportion of
economically active population in the late 1970s

3 – 4%

4.1 – 5%

5.1 – 6%

above 6%

data not available

Source: Statistical yearbooks of individual countries

GREENLAND

ICELAND

NORWAY
SWEDEN

DENMARK

IRELAND
UNITED
KINGDOM
N
B
GERMANY
W
E
CZEC
FRANCE
S
AUST
ITALY
YUGO
PORTUGAL
SPAIN
AL

TUNISIA

MOROCCO
ALGERIA
L

CANADA

UNITED STATES OF AMERICA

MAURITANIA
MALI
NIGER

MEXICO
inset
BAHAMAS

CUBA

JAMAICA

HAITI
DOMINICAN REPUBLIC
PUERTO RICO

SENEGAL
GAMBIA
GUINEA-BISSAU
UPPER
VOLTA
GUINEA

GUATEMALA
HONDURAS
EL SALVADOR
NICARAGUA

COSTA RICA

PANAMA

GRENADA
BARBADOS
TRINIDAD AND TOBAGO

VENEZUELA
GUYANA
SURINAM

SIERRA LEONE
LIBERIA
IVORY
COAST
GHANA
TOGO
BENIN
NIGERIA

EQUATORIAL
GUINEA
CAMEROON

GABON
CONG

COLOMBIA

ECUADOR

PERU

BOLIVIA

BRAZIL

PARAGUAY

ARGENTINA
URUGUAY

Continual military intervention

CHILE

AN

NAM

MEXICO

CUBA

GUATEMALA
HONDURAS
EL SALVADOR
NICARAGUA

COSTA RICA
PANAMA

COLOMBIA

UNION OF SOVIET SOCIALIST REPUBLICS

MONGOLIA

CHINA

N KOREA
S
JAPAN

TURKEY

CYPRUS
LEBANON SYRIA
ISRAEL IRAQ

AFGHANISTAN

IRAN

PAKISTAN

BHUTAN

NEPAL

TAIWAN

HONG KONG

KUWAIT
BAHRAIN
QATAR
U.A.E.
OMAN

EGYPT

SAUDI
ARABIA

INDIA

BURMA

THAILAND

PHILIPPINES

YEMEN
N S

KAM

UDAN

ETHIOPIA

SOMALIA

BANGLADESH

SRI LANKA

MALAYSIA

SINGAPORE

KENYA

RWANDA

BURUNDI

TANZANIA

COMOROS

INDONESIA

PAPUA
NEW GUINEA

MALAWI

MADAGASCAR

BIA

MBABWE

MOZAMBIQUE

H
A

AUSTRALIA

Military rule at the end of 1978

regimes governing by
martial law

military regimes

regimes with substantial
military participation

all other regimes

regime (as at the end of 1978)
established by military coup

military coup since 1960

further military intervention
since 1960

NEW ZEALAND

Source: A. S. Banks ed. Political Handbook
of the World, 1979

GREENLAND

ICELAND

IRELAND

UNITED
KINGDOM

CANADA

NO

NE
BEL
GER
CZ
AUS

FRANCE

ITALY

PORTUGAL

SPAIN

TUNISIA

UNITED STATES OF AMERICA

MOROCCO

ALGERIA

LI

MEXICO

CUBA
JAMAICA
HONDURAS
HAITI

DOMINICAN REPUBLIC

MAURITANIA

NIGER

GUATEMALA
EL SALVADOR

NICARAGUA
PANAMA

SENEGAL
GAMBIA
GUINEA-BISSAU

MALI
UPPER
VOLTA

COSTA RICA

TRINIDAD AND TOBAGO

GUINEA

SIERRA LEONE
LIBERIA

IVORY
COAST

NIGERIA

VENEZUELA

GUYANA

COLOMBIA

GHANA

BENIN
TOGO

CAMEROON

EQUATORIAL GUINEA

ECUADOR

GABON
CONGO

BRAZIL

AN

PERU

NAM

BOLIVIA

PARAGUAY

Soldiers and teachers

Ratio between soldiers and teachers in 1974

ARGENTINA

BAHRAIN

URUGUAY

more than 250 soldiers per 100 teachers

176-250 soldiers per 100 teachers

LUXEMBOURG

126-175 soldiers per 100 teachers

CHILE

100-125 soldiers/teachers
per 100 teachers/soldiers

MALTA

126-175 teachers per 100 soldiers

176-250 teachers per 100 soldiers

more than 250 teachers per 100 soldiers

FALKLAND ISLANDS

SINGAPORE

data not available

Source: Ruth L. Sivard, World Military and Social Expenditures,
Leesburg, Va., WMFE Publication, 1977

UNION OF SOVIET SOCIALIST REPUBLICS

MONGOLIA

JAPAN

KOREA
N
S

TURKEY

see inset 1

IRAQ

KUWAIT

IRAN

AFGHANISTAN

PAKISTAN

CHINA

TAIWAN

EGYPT

SAUDI
ARABIA

see inset 2

BHUTAN

NEPAL

INDIA

BANGLADESH

BURMA

N VIETNAM

LAOS

THAILAND

KAM

S VIETNAM

PHILIPPINES

SRI LANKA

MALAYSIA

SUDAN

ETHIOPIA

SOMALIA

UGANDA

KENYA

TANZANIA

MALAWI

ZIMBABWE

MOZAMBIQUE

MADAGASCAR

INDONESIA

PAPUA
NEW GUINEA

inset 1

CYPRUS

LEBANON

SYRIA

ISRAEL

JORDAN

inset 2

QATAR
UNITED ARAB EMIRATES

OMAN

N YEMEN

S YEMEN

AUSTRALIA

Soldiers

Soldiers per 1000 population in 1974

Soldier = all members of armed forces
Where data available

1 — 2.5   2.6 — 5   5.1 — 15   over 15

Extreme range: Niger 0.45 — United Arab Emirates 56

NEW ZEALAND

Military service
and conscientious objection

**Military service for men
mid 1970s**

compulsory

▓ (dark)	24 months and above
▓ (mid)	12 — 23 months
▓ (light)	below 12 months
⧄	compulsory but selective
▒	voluntary
>>>	reserve duty
☐	data not available

**Conscientious objection status
early 1970s**

🕊🕊	recognised
🔫	formally recognised but severely restricted
▬	not recognised

Source: International Institute of Strategic Studies
Schaffer & Weissbrodt, 'Conscientious objection to military
service as a human right', International Commission of
Jurists Review no. 9, December 1972

CANADA

UNITED STATES OF AMERICA

MEXICO

BAHAMAS
CUBA
JAMAICA HAITI DOMINICAN REPUBLIC
GUATEMALA HONDURAS
EL SALVADOR
NICARAGUA
COSTA RICA
PANAMA
GRENADA BARBADOS
TRINIDAD AND TOBAGO
VENEZUELA
GUYANA
SURINAM
COLOMBIA
ECUADOR
PERU
BRAZIL
BOLIVIA
PARAGUAY
CHILE
ARGENTINA
URUGUAY

BAHRAIN

FIJI

SWEDEN
FIN
NORWAY
DENMARK
IRELAND
UNITED
KINGDOM
NETHERLANDS
POLAND
BELGIUM GERMANY
(EAST)
GERMANY
(WEST)
CZECHOSLOVAKIA
FRANCE AUSTRIA HUNGAR
SWITZ
YUGOSLAV
PORTUGAL SPAIN
ITALY

TUNISIA
MOROCCO ALGERIA
LIBY
MAURITANIA MALI NIGER
CH
SENEGAL
GAMBIA
UPPER
GUINEA VOLTA
SIERRA LEONE IVORY
COAST GHANA NIGERIA
LIBERIA TOGO
BENIN
CAMEROON
EQUATORIAL GUINEA
GABON
CONGO
ANG
NAMIE

UNION OF SOVIET SOCIALIST REPUBLICS

MONGOLIA

CHINA

N KOREA
S

JAPAN

TURKEY
SYRIA
CYPRUS
LEBANON
IRAQ
AFGHANISTAN
ISRAEL JORDAN
KUWAIT
IRAN
PAKISTAN
BHUTAN
NEPAL
inset
EGYPT
BAHRAIN
QATAR
U.A.E.
OMAN
SAUDI
ARABIA
INDIA
B-
DESH BURMA
TAIWAN
HONG KONG
LAOS
VIETNAM
SUDAN
N S YEMEN
THAILAND
KAM
PHILIPPINES
ETHIOPIA
SRI LANKA
SOMALIA
UGANDA
KENYA
RWANDA
BURUNDI
TANZANIA
MALAYSIA
SINGA-
PORE
INDONESIA
PAPUA
NEW GUINEA
BIA
MALAWI
ZIMBABWE
MADAGASCAR
MOZAMBIQUE
Whites
only
SWAZILAND
LESOTHO
TH
CA

TURKEY
SYRIA
CYPRUS
LEBANON
IRAQ
ISRAEL
SAUDI
ARABIA
JORDAN
inset

AUSTRALIA

NEW ZEALAND

Capital punishment and state assassination

CANADA

UNITED STATES OF AMERICA

MEXICO

GUATEMALA
EL SALVADOR
HONDURAS
NICARAGUA
COSTA RICA
PANAMA

CUBA
BAHAMAS
JAMAICA
HAITI
DOMINICAN REPUBLIC
PUERTO RICO
BARBADOS
TRINIDAD AND TOBAGO
GUYANA
SURINAM

COLOMBIA
VENEZUELA
ECUADOR
PERU
BRAZIL
BOLIVIA
PARAGUAY
CHILE
ARGENTINA
URUGUAY

NORWAY
SWEDEN
FIN
DENMARK
IRELAND
UNITED KINGDOM
NETHER-LANDS
BELG IUM
LUXEMBOURG
GERMANY WEST
EAST
POLAN
CZECHOSLOVAK
AUSTRIA
HUN
FRANCE
SWITZ
ITALY
YUGOSLA
PORTUGAL
SPAIN
ALBA

TUNISIA
MOROCCO
ALGERIA
L
MAURITANIA
MALI
NIGER
SENEGAL
GAMBIA
UPPER VOLTA
GUINEA
NIGERIA
SIERRA LEONE
IVORY COAST
LIBERIA
CAMEROON
GHANA
TOGO
EQUATORIAL GUINEA
GABON
BENIN
CONGO
AN
NAM

Prisoners per 100,000 population
1974 or nearest year

- over 150
- 101 — 150
- 51 — 100
- 50 and below
- data not available

Extreme range: USA 189 — Kampuchea 9

Capital punishment and state assassination

Death penalty, as of May 1979
Where data available

- in force
- retained, but suspended in practice 1977-79
- abolished in time of peace only
- abolished for all offences

Source: Fifth UN Congress on the Prevention of Crime and the
Treatment of Offenders, Working Paper, 1975
Amnesty International Reports, 1977, 1978, 1979

Source: Amnesty International Report, The Death Penalty
Amnesty International, The Death Penalty,
(addenda and update) 1979

UNION OF SOVIET SOCIALIST REPUBLICS

MONGOLIA

CHINA

JAPAN

TURKEY

IRAN

AFGHAN ISTAN

PAKISTAN

INDIA

NEPAL

BURMA

VIETNAM

LAOS

TAIWAN

HONG KONG

KOREA

N   S

SAUDI ARABIA

OMAN

QATAR

U.A.E

KUWAIT

S YEMEN

N Y

DJIBOUTI

ETHIOPIA

SOMALIA

KENYA

UGANDA

RWANDA

TANZANIA

MALAWI

MOZAMBIQUE

ZIMBABWE

MADAGASCAR

SOUTH FRICA

SWAZILAND

LESOTHO

SUDAN

EGYPT

BANGLADESH

SRI LANKA

THAILAND

KAM

MALAYSIA

SINGAPORE

INDONESIA

PHILIPPINES

PAPUA NEW GUINEA

AUSTRALIA

inset

TURKEY

CYPRUS

SYRIA

LEBANON

ISRAEL

JORDAN

IRAQ

SAUDI ARABIA

inset

Political prisoners and torture

Political prisoners and torture reported 1977-79
Where data available

| | political prisoners |

| | torture widely used and officially condoned |

Absence of information may only mean that the
scourge in question has not been reported

NEW ZEALAND

CYPRUS

SYRIA

LEB

IRAQ

inset

IRELAND
UNITED KINGDOM
NETH WEST EAST POLAND
BEL GERMANY
CZECH
FRANCE SWITZ AUSTRIA HUNGARY
ITALY ROMANIA
YUGOSLAVIA
ALBANIA BULGARIA
GREECE
TURKEY
CYPRUS
LEBANON SYRIA
ISRAEL
JOR

UNION OF SOVIET SOCIALIST REPUBLI

inset 1   75

1945

122,000

300,000
1975 est.

IRA
13
19

46,000 1975
from Vietnam

100,000 + 1976 —
from Argentina

120,000 + 1975
from Mozambique

420,000 + 1975

PORTUGAL
SPAIN

MOROCCO

82,000
1977

ALGERIA   LIBYA   EGYPT

SAUDI ARABIA

KUWAIT
BAHRAIN
QAT

MAURITANIA

MALI   NIGER   CHAD   SUDAN

600,000
1979 est.

N
YEMEN

20,000
1978 est.

CAPE VERDE

SENEGAL
GAMBIA
GUINEA-BISSAU
GUINEA

UPPER
VOLTA

NIGERIA

CENTRAL AFRICAN
REPUBLIC

250,000
1977 —

100,000
1979 est.

ETHIOPIA

DJIBOUTI 200,000
1978

500,000
1977 —

SOMALIA

1,200,000
1977 —

SIERRA LEONE
LIBERIA

IVORY
COAST

GHANA
TOGO
BENIN

75,000 1976

30-35,000
1979 est.

EQUATORIAL GUINEA
CAMEROON

80,000
1979 est.

GABON
CONGO

ZAIRE

500,000
1976 est.

inset 2

UGANDA
RWANDA
BURUNDI

25,000

265,000
1979 est.

KENYA

167,000
1979 est.

TANZANIA

COMOROS

16,000
1976 — 77

CANADA

220,000 1975
from Vietnam

UNITED STATES
OF AMERICA

MEXICO

BAHAMAS

15,000
mid 1970's

CUB

HAITI

DOMINICAN REPUBLIC
PUERTO RICO

2,500 from
L. America

16,000 from L. America
Europe
1979 est.

GUATEMALA
EL SALVADOR

HOND
NIC

100,000 1979 est.

COSTA RICA
PANAMA

TRINIDAD AND TOBAGO

VENEZUELA

GUYANA
SURINAM

COLOMBIA

1,500
from L. America

ECUADOR

PERU

BRAZIL

BOLIVIA

180,000
1972

700,000
1975 —

ANGOLA

ZAMBIA

100,000
1979 est.

58,000

MALAWI

22,000
1978 est.

ZIMBABWE

150,000 1978 est.
MOZAMBIQUE

1,000,000 1978 est.

MADAGASCAR

NAMIBIA

20,000
1979 est.

BOTSWANA

SWAZILAND

3,400 1979 est.

LESOTHO

SOUTH
AFRICA

150,000 from Chile
1973 —
to Australia
New Zealand
Europe
L. America
USA

PARAG

CHILE

URUGUAY

ARGENTINA

23,000
from
Europe
7,000
from
L. America

MONGOLIA

N KOREA

S KOREA

JAPAN

CHINA

TAIWAN

AFGHANISTAN

380,000
1978

PAKISTAN

11,000 1974

121,500 1974

108,750 1974

NEPAL

BHUTAN

BURMA

250,000
1975 —

130,000
1979 only

HONG KONG

167,000
1978

VIETNAM

450,000 1979 est

62,300
1975

INDIA

BANGLADESH

50,000
1979 est.

100,000

138,000
1975 —

LAOS 3,500,000 1979 est.

KAMPUCHEA

540,000
1979 est.

140,000

6,300 1979 est.

PHILIPPINES

SRI LANKA

THAILAND

76,000 1975

MALAYSIA

SINGAPORE

40,700
1975 —

INDONESIA

20,000 1975 —

PAPUA NEW GUINEA

AUSTRALIA

set 1

TURKEY

9,000
1974

500,000
1979 est.

SYRIA

204,000
1979 est.

CYPRUS

LEBANON
700,000
1979 est.

220,000
1979 est.
ISRAEL
00 to
Strip

IRAQ

JORDAN

318,000 to west bank
1979 est.

79 est.

700,000 1979 est.

EGYPT

SAUDI ARABIA

set 2

UGANDA

KENYA

112,000
1979 est.

ZAIRE

RWANDA
10,000 1973

BURUNDI

,000
973

40,000 1973

500,000
1973

TANZANIA

Numbers of new refugees 1972-79
including residual Palestinian refugee population

over 300,000

150,000 — 300,000

50,000 — 150,000

below 50,000

population internally displaced 1972-79

*Source: Minority Rights Group
Keesings Contemporary Archives
Press reports*

NEW ZEALAND

CANADA

UNITED STATES OF AMERICA

MEXICO

BAHAMAS **E**

CUBA
E JAMAICA
BELIZE
GUATEMALA **S**
HONDURAS
EL SALVADOR
NICARAGUA
COSTA RICA
PANAMA

HAITI **F**
DOMINICAN REPUBLIC
PUERTO RICO **E**

BARBADOS **E**
TRINIDAD AND TOBAGO **E**

VENEZUELA
COLOMBIA
GUYANA **E**
SURINAM **D**
FRENCH GUIANA **F**

ECUADOR **S**
PERU **S**

BRAZIL

BOLIVIA **S**
PARAGUAY **S**

CHILE

ARGENTINA

URUGUAY

FALKLAND ISLANDS

NORWAY
SWEDEN
FINLAND
DENMARK
IRELAND **It**
UNITED KINGDOM
NETHERLANDS
BELGIUM
WEST GERMANY
EAST GERMANY
POLAND
CZECHOSLOVAKIA
FRANCE
SWITZ.
AUSTRIA
HUNGARY
ITALY
YUGOSLAVIA
PORTUGAL
SPAIN **S**
S
S
ALBANIA
I

TUNISIA
MOROCCO
ALGERIA **F**
LIBYA

MAURITANIA
MALI **F**
NIGER **F**
CAPE VERDE **P**
SENEGAL **F**
GAMBIA **E**
GUINEA-BISSAU **P**
GUINEA **F**
UPPER VOLTA **F**
NIGERIA **E**
SIERRA LEONE **E**
IVORY COAST **F**
GHANA
BENIN
F
TOGO **F**
CAMEROON **E/F**
LIBERIA **E**
EQUATORIAL GUINEA **S**
SAO TOME **P**
GABON **F**
CONGO **F**
ANG
NAMI
Af/

E FIJI

F **E** MAURITIUS

E/F SEYCHELLES

E WESTERN SAMOA

Official language or languages

not the languages of the majority

spoken by the majority but not by many of the poor

spoken by most people in creole form

widely spoken throughout country or in appropriate region

old imperial language or languages, not official, but still used in government and business

★ countries with significant linguistic conflict

A language of rule is one which is used by the governing classes, and which helps to secure their dominance

UNION OF SOVIET SOCIALIST REPUBLICS

R

MONGOLIA

R

inset TURKEY
SYRIA

Fa

AFGHANISTAN
IRAN   Fa
IRAQ
KUWAIT
EGYPT
QATAR
UAE
SAUDI ARABIA
OMAN
N S YEMEN
YEMEN
DJIBOUTI

CHINA
Pu

N KOREA
S KOREA

JAPAN

TAIWAN

HONG KONG E
MACAO P

PAKISTAN
U

INDIA
H/E

NEPAL
B H
B DESH
BURMA

LAOS
THAILAND
VIETNAM
KAM

PHILIPPINES
T E/S

SRI LANKA

BRUNEI

MALAYSIA

E SINGAPORE

In INDONESIA

PAPUA NEW GUINEA
E

SUDAN

A/E
ETHIOPIA
Am
SOMALIA

E
Sw
KENYA
UGANDA E
RWANDA F
BURUNDI F
MALAWI E
COMOROS F
E
TANZANIA

P
MOZAMBIQUE

MADAGASCAR
F

MBABWE E

SWAZILAND E
LESOTHO E

inset

E
CYPRUS
F/E LEBANON
SYRIA

ISRAEL Heb

JORDAN

AUSTRALIA

Languages

Afrikaans	**Af**	Bahasa Indonesia	**In**
Amharic	**Am**	Irish Gaelic	**Ir**
Arabic	**A**	Italian	**I**
Dutch	**D**	Portuguese	**P**
English	**E**	Putonghua	**Pu**
Farsi	**Fa**	Russian	**R**
French	**F**	Spanish	**S**
German	**G**	Swahili	**Sw**
Hebrew	**Heb**	Tagalog	**T**
Hindi	**H**	Urdu	**U**

Source: Europa Yearbook 1978
Statesman's Yearbook 1977, 1978, 1979,
US. CIA National Basic Intelligence Factbook
Private sources

NEW ZEALAND

CANADA

UNITED STATES OF AMERICA

MEXICO

BAHAMAS

CUBA

JAMAICA

HAITI

DOMINICAN REPUBLIC
PUERTO RICO

GUATEMALA
EL SALVADOR

HONDURAS

NICARAGUA

COSTA RICA

PANAMA

TRINIDAD AND TOBAGO

VENEZUELA

COLOMBIA

GUYANA

SURINAM

FRENCH GUIANA

ECUADOR

PERU

BRAZIL

BOLIVIA

PARAGUAY

CHILE

URUGUAY

ARGENTINA

NORWAY

SWEDEN

FINLAND

DENMARK

IRELAND

UNITED
KINGDOM

POLAND

BELG

WEST
GERMANY

EAST

CZECHOSLOVAKIA

LUXEMBOURG

AUSTRIA

HUNGARY

ROM

FRANCE

SWITZ

ITALY

YUGOSLAVIA

PORTUGAL

SPAIN

Rome

ALBANIA

GREE

TUNISIA

MOROCCO

ALGERIA

LIB

MAURITANIA

MALI

NIGER

C

SENEGAL

GAMBIA

GUINEA-BISSAU

GUINEA

UPPER
VOLTA

NIGERIA

SIERRA LEONE

IVORY
COAST

GHANA

BENIN

TOGO

CEN
AFR
RE

LIBERIA

CAMEROON

EQUATORIAL
GUINEA

GABON

CONGO

AN

NAM

BAHRAIN

BARBADOS

BRUNEI

FIJI

ICELAND

MALTA

MAURITIUS

REUNION

WESTERN SAMOA

Animism

Buddhism

Shintoism

Christianity

Christianity
(no dominant sect)

Catholicism

Protestantism

other Christianity
(Orthodox, Maronite etc.)

Hinduism

Islam

Sunni

Shi'ism and sub-sects

Judaism

Marxism-Leninism

Moscow denomination

Peking denomination

Moscow alignment

local variant

■ Holy capitals

★ site of recent
religious conflict

Source: Europa, Middle East and North Africa Yearbook 1979-80
Europa, Africa South of the Sahara Yearbook 1978-79
Europa, The Far East and Australasia Yearbook 1978-79
C. Veliz (ed). Latin America and the Caribbean: a Handbook, 1968
Statistical Yearbook of the Netherlands, 1978
Private sources

A religion of rule is one which is professed by the governing classes and which sustains their solidarity

UNION OF SOVIET SOCIALIST REPUBLICS

■Moscow

MONGOLIA

URKEY
inset 1

YPRUS
SYRIA
LEBANON
ISRAEL JOR
IRAQ
IRAN
AFGHANISTAN

PAKISTAN

YPT

DAN

inset 2
KUWAIT

■Medina
■Mecca
SAUDI ARABIA
N YEMEN
S YEMEN
OMAN

DJIBOUTI

ETHIOPIA
SOMALIA

KENYA

TANZANIA

LAWI

MOZAMBIQUE

CHINA

Peking ■

N KOREA
S KOREA
JAPAN
■Ise

TAIWAN

NEPAL
BHUTAN
Benares ■
Gaya ■
B-DESH
BURMA
INDIA

LAO
THAILAND
KAMP
VIETNAM

PHILIPPINES

SRI LANKA

MALAYSIA

INDONESIA

PAPUA NEW GUINEA

AUSTRALIA

inset 1

SYRIA
CYPRUS
LEBANON
ISRAEL
Jerusalem
JORDAN

inset 2

KUWAIT
QATAR
UNITED ARAB EMIRATES
OMAN
SAUDI ARABIA
S YEMEN
N YEMEN

NEW ZEALAND

Big money

NEW ZEALAND

AUSTRALIA

PAPUA NEW GUINEA

JAPAN

N KOREA

S

TAIWAN

PHILIPPINES

VIETNAM

KAM

THAILAND

MALAYSIA

INDONESIA

BURMA

MONGOLIA

CHINA

NEPAL

BANGLADESH

INDIA

SRI LANKA

UNION OF SOVIET SOCIALIST REPUBLICS

AFGH

PAKISTAN

IRAN

KUWAIT

IRAQ

TURKEY

SY

CYPRUS

GREECE

SAUDI ARABIA

OMAN

YEMS YEMEN

SOMALIA

MADAGASCAR

EGYPT

SUDAN

ETHIOPIA

UG

KENYA

TANZ

MOZAMBIQUE

FINLAND

NORWAY

SWEDEN

DEN

N

POL

CZ

GER

HUN

YUGO

ROM

BUL

AUST

ITALY

FRANCE

SPAIN

PORTUGAL

IRELAND

UNITED KINGDOM

ICELAND

MOROCCO

TUNISIA

LIBYA

ALGERIA

NIGER

CHAD

C A R

ZAIRE

CAM

GABON

CO

ANGOLA

ZAMBIA

ZIMB

BOTS

NAMIBIA

SOUTH AFRICA

MALI

MAURITANIA

SENEGAL

GAMBIA

GUINEA-BISSAU

GUINEA

SIERRA LEONE

LIBERIA

IVORY CO

VOLTA

GHANA

TOGO

BENIN

NIGERIA

GREENLAND

National reserves compared with assets of banks at the end of 1976

reserves below Bank of America, but above National Westminster Bank ($29,080 million) the 20th in size

reserves below National Westminster, but above Hong Kong & Shanghai Banking Corporation ($14,188 million) the 75th in size

reserves below Hong Kong & Shanghai Banking Corporation, but above Bank of Hiroshima ($4,822 million) the 150th in size

reserves below Bank of Hiroshima but above Cantonal Bank of St. Gall ($1,707 million) the 300th in size

reserves below Cantonal Bank of St. Gall

data not available

No state has reserves above the assets of The Bank of America ($73,913 million), the world's largest bank

FALKLAND ISLANDS

BRAZIL

URUGUAY

ARGENTINA

PARAG

BOLIVIA

CHILE

PERU

ECUADOR

COLOMBIA

VENEZUELA

GUYANA

SURINAM

TRINIDAD AND TOBAGO

DOMINICAN REPUBLIC

HAITI

JAMAICA

CUBA

BAHAMAS

BELIZE

GUATEMALA

EL SALVADOR

NICARAGUA

COSTA RICA

PANAMA

MEXICO

UNITED STATES OF AMERICA

CANADA

Source:
International Financial Statistics 1977
The Banker, July 1977

35. The Public and the Private

Big business

National incomes (1977 GNPs) compared with
sales incomes of US multinationals in 1977

GNP greater than income of Exxon ($44.8 billion)
top US industrial company

GNP below income of Exxon, but above that of
Mobil ($26.062 billion) the **5th** in size

GPN below income of Mobil, but above that of
Chrysler ($11.7 billion) the 10th in size

GNP below income of Chrysler, but above that of
Coca Cola ($2.87 billion) the 64th in size

GNP below income of Coca Cola, but above that of
Time Inc. ($0.91 billion) the 221st in size

GNP below that of Time Inc.

data not available

Source:
World Bank Atlas 1977
Fortune, May 1977

CANADA

UNITED STATES OF AMERICA

MEXICO

BAHAMAS

CUBA

JAMAICA HAITI DOMINICAN REPUBLIC
PUERTO RICO

GUATEMALA HONDURAS
EL SALVADOR
NICARAGUA NETHERLANDS ANTILLES BARBADOS
COSTA RICA TRINIDAD AND TOBAGO
PANAMA VENEZUELA GUYANA
COLOMBIA SURINAM

ECUADOR

PERU

BRAZIL

BOLIVIA

PARAGUAY

CHILE

URUGUAY

ARGENTINA

**Transnationals with sales of
more than US $1 billion
at the end of 1976**

- $1b — 1.99b
- $2b — 3.99b
- $4b — 5.99b
- $6b — 7.99b
- $8 billion and over

Source: UN Centre on Transnational Corporations,
Transnational Corporations in World Development,
UNESCO 1978

NORWAY

DENMARK

WEST GERMANY SWE

IRELAND NETHERLANDS

UNITED KINGDOM EAST GERMANY

BELGIUM AUS

FRANCE SWITZ

ITALY

PORTUGAL SPAIN

MOROCCO

ALGERIA L

MAURITANIA MALI NIGER

SENEGAL
GAMBIA
GUINEA UPPER VOLTA NIGERIA
SIERRA LEONE IVORY COAST GHANA BENIN
LIBERIA TOGO CAMEROON
C

Source: UN Centre on Transnational Corporations,
Transnational Corporations in World Development,
UNESCO 1978

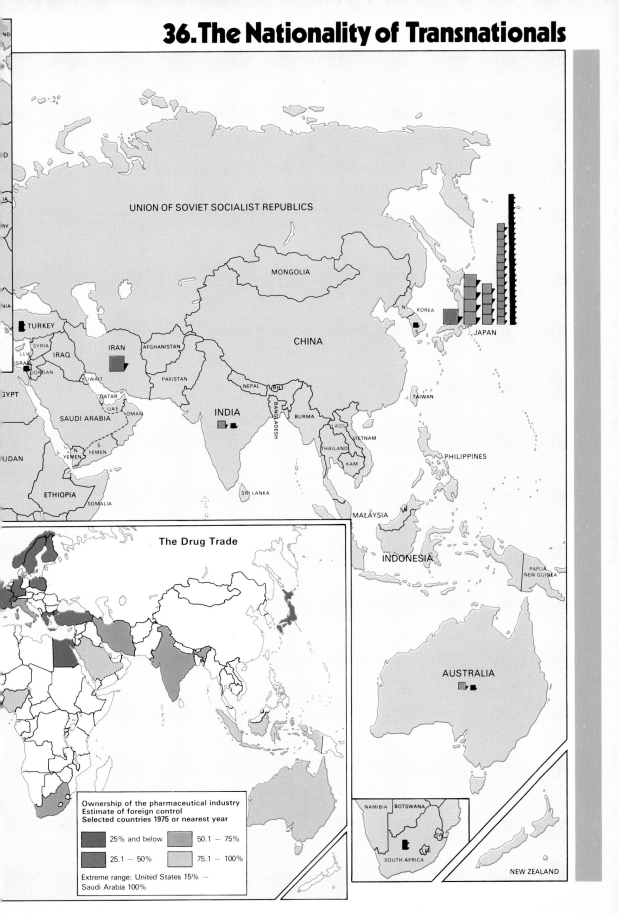

UNION OF SOVIET SOCIALIST REPUBLICS

MONGOLIA

CHINA

TURKEY

SYRIA
LEB
ISRAEL
JORDAN
IRAQ
KUWAIT
IRAN
AFGHANISTAN

QATAR
UAE
OMAN

SAUDI ARABIA

PAKISTAN

NEPAL
BH
BANGLADESH
INDIA
BURMA

N
YEMEN
S
YEMEN

ETHIOPIA

SOMALIA

SRI LANKA

KOREA
N
S
JAPAN

TAIWAN

LAOS
VIETNAM
THAILAND
KAM

PHILIPPINES

MALAYSIA

INDONESIA

PAPUA
NEW GUINEA

AUSTRALIA

NEW ZEALAND

The Drug Trade

NAMIBIA BOTSWANA
SW
LES
SOUTH AFRICA

Ownership of the pharmaceutical industry
Estimate of foreign control
Selected countries 1975 or nearest year

25% and below	50.1 — 75%
25.1 — 50%	75.1 — 100%

Extreme range: United States 15% —
Saudi Arabia 100%

TURKEY

LEBANON
SYRIA
ISRAEL JORDAN
IRAN

BAHRAIN
U.A.E. **t**

S. YEMEN

INDIA

SRI LANKA

T
MALDIVE

S KOREA

TAIWAN

T MACAO HONG KONG

Hong Kong 13

THAILAND

t

T
BRUNEI

MALAYSIA

SINGAPORE

INDONESIA

PHILIPPINES

UNITED ST

MEXICO

GUA
EL SA

Hong Ke

US

Gre

N.

W. Gerr

Sv

Ita

Ne

UK

O MAURITIUS

flags of convenience, 1978

W. Germany 145

Japan 75

Switzerland 53   Hong Kong 28

UK 31   Greece 17   Norway 12

NETHERLANDS ANTILLES

NICARAGUA

JAMAICA

HAITI

PUERTO RICO

Tax havens and Flags of convenience

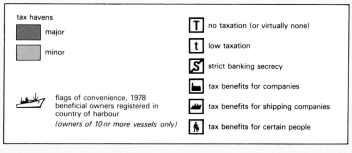

tax havens

major

minor

flags of convenience, 1978
beneficial owners registered in
country of harbour
(owners of 10 or more vessels only)

T   no taxation (or virtually none)

t   low taxation

S   strict banking secrecy

tax benefits for companies

tax benefits for shipping companies

tax benefits for certain people

ISLE OF MAN

UNITED KINGDOM

GUERNSEY JERSEY

SWITZERLAND

LIECHTENSTEIN

LUXEMBOURG

MONACO

ANDORRA

GREECE

Greece 475

W. Germany 52

CYPRUS

MALTA

TUNISIA

MOROCCO

EGYPT

AMERICA

BERMUDA

Canada 47

USA 11

BAHAMAS

CAYMAN

USA 11

TURKS AND CAICOS

HAITI

DOMINICAN REPUBLIC

VIRGIN ISLANDS

ANGUILLA

PUERTO RICO

ANTIGUA

JAMAICA

ST. LUCIA

NETH. ANTILLES

BARBADOS

GRENADA

TRINIDAD AND TOBAGO

VENEZUELA

COLOMBIA

PANAMA

DURAS

RAGUA

ICA

SENEGAL

IVORY COAST

GHANA

TOGO

LIBERIA

USA 576

Greece 571

H. Kong 550   Norway 38

Japan 168   Israel 37

W. Germany 72 Italy 37

Switz. 84   Neths 30   Canada 14

UK 53   Monaco 23   N. Korea 14

BRAZIL

CUADOR

URU

HEBRIDES

CHILE

URUGUAY

ERN SAMOA

BOTSWANA

SWAZILAND

LESOTHO

SOUTH AFRICA

Production zones

free production zones

major

minor

offshore manufacturing zones

major

minor

under construction 1975

Sources:
UNCTAD, Handbook of International Trade
and Development Statistics, 1979
B. Spitz, Tax Havens Encyclopedia, 1978
Froebel, Heinrichs & Kreye,
The New International Division of Labour, 1980
Private sources

CANADA

UNITED STATES OF AMERICA

+3%

3,000,000

MEXICO

NORWAY

total
28,000
DENM

total
76,000

IRELAND

UK

others

Ireland
452,000

others
948,000

UNITED
KINGDOM

+7%

Italy
72,000

Spain
37,000

Greece
50,000

Spain
34,000

NETHERLANDS
+4.7%

BELGIUM
+7.1%

others
36,000
total
26,400

WE
GERM
+9.

Morocco
30,000

Italy
90,000

Portugal
85,000

L

FRANCE

+11%

Spain
165,000

SWITZER-
LAND

Morocco
16,000

others
176,000

Italy
230,000

Be

SPAIN   -4.7%

PORTUGAL

-14.2%

W. Germany

France

others

Belgium

W. Germany

France

UK

Switzerland

others

Portugal
475,000

Spain
265,000

Morocco
130,000

Tunisia
70,000

Algeria
440,000

Yugoslavia
50,000

Total numbers of foreign workers
in the mid 1970s

arrivals   departures

below 100,000

100,000 – 200,000

200,000 – 300,000

300,000 – 400,000

400,000 – 600,000

over 600,000

Countries of labour immigration

Countries of labour emigration

Worker migrants as a proportion of:

the host (+) country's labour force

the home (-) country's labour force

Source: Minority Rights Group 1978
Government statistical yearbooks
UN, World Population Trends and Policies, 1977
Private sources

MOROCCO

Belgium

France

others

ALGERIA

France

others

TU

W. G

© Copyright Pluto Press

SWEDEN

Finland
187,800

Yugoslavia
40,000

UNION OF SOVIET
SOCIALIST REPUBLICS

POLAND

EAST GERMANY

others
1,000

Yugoslavia

Turkey

590,000

CZECHOSLOVAKIA

Greece

AUSTRIA

225,000
to Switzerland

HUNGARY

Italy
32,000

ROMANIA

5.6%

YUGOSLAVIA -8.5%

others ← France ←

W. Germany ← Sweden ←

BULGARIA

W.Germany

France

UK

total
26,000

Switzerland

others

ALBANIA

GREECE -7.8%

W. Germany ←

UK ←

others ←

TURKEY -4.5%

W. Germany ←

others ←

LIBYA

+16%

MAURITANIA

SENEGAL

GAMBIA

GUINEA-BISSAU

SIERRA LEONE

LIBERIA

GUINEA

MALI

NIGER

1,400,000 from U. Volta,
Mali, Guinea, Niger

150,000

IVORY COAST
+55%

GHANA
+24%

TOGO

BENIN

NIGERIA

900,000 from
Togo,
U. Volta, others

CAMEROON

NAMIBIA

BOTSWANA
-12%

MALAWI -3.5%

79,000

MOZAMBIQUE -4.5%

34,000

-8%

SWAZILAND

138,000

10,000

129,000

from Mozambique

SOUTH AFRICA
+5%

LESOTHO -29%

SYRIA

LEBANON

ISRAEL

JORDAN

IRAQ

IRAN

KUWAIT
+80%

213,000

343,000

400

22,400

BAHRAIN

QATAR

LIBYA
+22%

EGYPT

118,000

SAUDI ARABIA
+50%

UNITED ARAB EMIRATES
+88%

OMAN

748,000

N YEMEN

S YEMEN

SUDAN

ETHIOPIA

SOMALIA

India ←

Bangladesh ←

Pakistan ←

S. Korea ←

Afghanistan ←

+37% Bahrain

+88% Qatar

UNION OF SOVIET SOCIALIST REPUBLICS

MONGOLIA

CHINA

N KOREA
S KOREA
JAPAN

TURKEY
inset

SYRIA IRAQ

IRAN

AFGHANISTAN

GYPT

PAKISTAN

SAUDI ARABIA

OMAN

KUWAIT

NEPAL

INDIA

BURMA

LAOS

HONG KONG

VIETNAM

PHILIPPINES

N YEM S YEMEN

SUDAN

ETHIOPIA

SOMALIA

BANGLADESH

KAM

THAILAND

UGANDA

KENYA

SRI LANKA

MALAYSIA

TANZANIA

MALAWI

SINGAPORE

INDONESIA

PAPUA NEW GUINEA

ZIMB

MOZAMBIQUE

MADAGASCAR

SWAZILAND

AUSTRALIA

inset

TURKEY

CYPRUS
LEBANON

SYRIA

IRAQ

ISRAEL

JORDAN

SAUDI
ARABIA

Levels of exploitation in manufacturing, 1970s

1st level   2nd level   3rd level   4th level   5th level
Where data available

Exploitation for this purpose is defined as:
gross output in manufacturing minus payroll in manufacturing
divided by payroll in manufacturing

NEW
ZEALAND

Source: UN Yearbooks of Industrial Statistics, 1978 and 1979 Vol. 1

Workers on the land

NEW ZEALAND

AUSTRALIA

PAPUA NEW GUINEA

JAPAN

KOREA S

TAIWAN

PHILIPPINES

VIETNAM

LAOS

KAM

THAILAND

BURMA

B'DESH

MALAYSIA

INDONESIA

SRI LANKA

INDIA

NEPAL

MONGOLIA

CHINA

UNION OF SOVIET SOCIALIST REPUBLICS

AFGH

PAKISTAN

IRAN

KUWAIT

IRAQ

SAUDI ARABIA

S YEMEN

OMAN

SOMALIA

ETHIOPIA

KENYA

TANZ

MOZAMBIQUE

MADAGASCAR

SUDAN

C A R

ZAIRE

ZAMBIA

ZIMB

BOTS

SOUTH AFRICA

NAMIBIA

ANGOLA

CON

GABON

CAM

CHAD

NIGER

NIGERIA

BENIN

TOGO

GHANA

IVORY CO

LIBERIA

SIERRA LEONE

GUINEA

GUINEA BISSAU

GAMBIA

SENEGAL

MAURITANIA

MALI

VOLTA

LIBYA

EGYPT

TUNISIA

ALGERIA

MOROCCO

TURKEY

CYPRUS

SY

GREECE

BUL

ROM

YUG

HUN

ITALY

AUT

POL

E GER

W GER

DEN

N

FRANCE

SPAIN

PORTUGAL

SWEDEN

NORWAY

FINLAND

IRELAND

UNITED KINGDOM

ICELAND

GREENLAND

CANADA

UNITED STATES OF AMERICA

MEXICO

GUATEMALA

EL SALVADOR

BELIZE

HONDURAS

NICARAGUA

COSTA RICA

PANAMA

JAMAICA

HAITI

CUBA

DOMINICAN REPUBLIC

BAHAMAS

TRINIDAD AND TOBAGO

VENEZUELA

COLOMBIA

ECUADOR

PERU

GUYANA

SURINAM

FRENCH GUIANA

BRAZIL

BOLIVIA

PARAG

URUGUAY

ARGENTINA

CHILE

FALKLAND ISLANDS

Proportion of economically active labour force in agriculture in mid 1970s

- over 60%
- 50.1 — 60%
- 40.1 — 50%
- 30.1 — 40%
- 20.1 — 30%
- 10.1 — 20%
- 10% and below
- data not available

Extreme range: 94.4% Nepal — 2.19% Singapore

BAHRAIN
BARBADOS
FIJI
HONG KONG
LUXEMBOURG
MALTA
MAURITIUS
SINGAPORE
SEYCHELLES
WESTERN SAMOA

Source:
ILO. Yearbook of Labour Statistics, 1979
ILO. Statistical Yearbook, 1977, 1978
UN. Statistical Yearbook, 1976
UN. Statistical Yearbook for Asia and the Pacific, 1977

Workers in industry

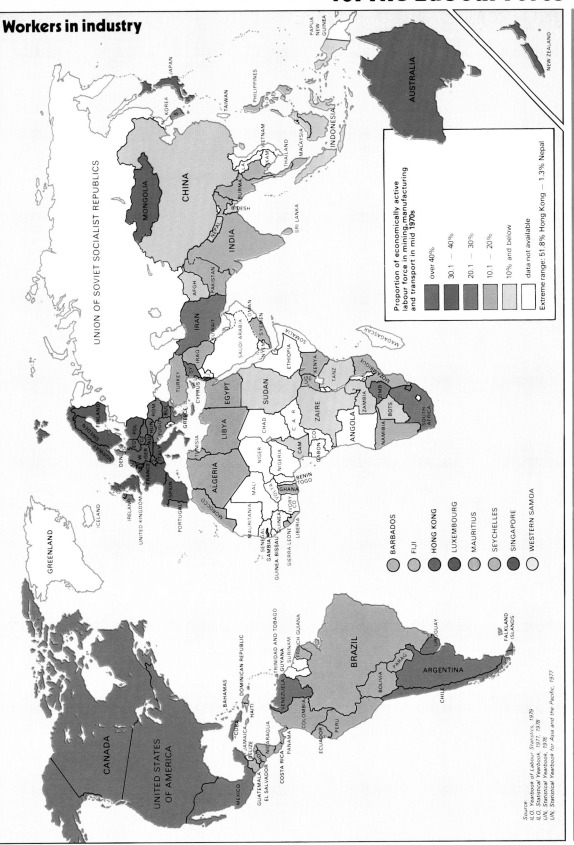

Proportion of economically active labour force in mining, manufacturing and transport in mid 1970s

over 40%

30.1 — 40%

20.1 — 30%

10.1 — 20%

10% and below

data not available

Extreme range: 51.8% Hong Kong — 1.3% Nepal

BARBADOS

FIJI

HONG KONG

LUXEMBOURG

MAURITIUS

SEYCHELLES

SINGAPORE

WESTERN SAMOA

Source
I.L.O. Yearbook of Labour Statistics, 1979
I.L.O. Statistical Yearbook, 1977, 1978
UN, Statistical Yearbook, 1976
UN, Statistical Yearbook for Asia and the Pacific, 1977

Sexual discrimination in jobs

5 Countries ranked from Bulgaria 1 (least discrimination) to Syria 94 (most discrimination) in 1976
Where data available

Index: the proportion of women (or men) who would have to change their occupational or industrial classification for there to be sex equality in jobs

Source: Elise Boulding et al, Handbook of International Data on Women 1976

Women as a proportion of the non-domestic labour force: latest year between 1975 and 1979

- over 40%
- 30.1 - 40%
- 20.1 - 30%
- 10.1 - 20%
- 10% and below
- data not available

Extreme range: Botswana 51.82% — Guinea-Bissau 3.61%

Source: ILO Yearbook of Labour Statistics 1978, 1979

UNION OF SOVIET SOCIALIST REPUBLICS

MONGOLIA

CHINA

TURKEY **93**

CYPRUS
84 SYRIA **94**
LEBANON IRAQ
ISRAEL JORDAN **39**
33

IRAN **64**

AFGHANISTAN

KUWAIT **57**

PAKISTAN **89**

BAHRAIN **51**
QATAR
U.A.E.

SAUDI
ARABIA

OMAN

N S. **88**
YEMEN YEMEN

EGYPT **50**

SUDAN

ETHIOPIA

SOMALIA

KENYA **71**

UGANDA
BURUNDI

TANZANIA **87**

COMOROS

MALAWI

MOZAMBIQUE

ZIMBABWE **5**

MADAGASCAR

MAURITIUS **19**

SWAZILAND **32**

LESOTHO

INDIA **63**

NEPAL **29** BHUTAN

B-DESH

BURMA

SRI LANKA **70**

THAILAND **85**

KAMPUCHEA **90**

VIETNAM

MALAYSIA
SINGAPORE **26**

BRUNEI

INDONESIA **67**

N. KOREA
S. **86**

JAPAN **73**

RYUKYU IS. **55**

TAIWAN

HONG KONG **23**

PHILIPPINES **59**

PAPUA
NEW GUINEA

AUSTRALIA **12**

NEW ZEALAND **34**

GREENLAND

ICELAND

NORWAY   SWE

DENMARK

CANADA

IRELAND   UNITED   GERMANY
           KINGDOM   E   F
                        N
                        W   CZ
FRANCE   S   AUS
                        YUGO
UNITED STATES OF AMERICA   PORTUGAL   SPAIN   ITA

                                                TUNISIA
MOROCCO

                                    ALGERIA   LIE

MEXICO   BAHAMAS

              CUBA   MAURITANIA
       BELIZE   DOMINICAN REPUBLIC   MALI   NIGER
GUATEMALA HONDURAS PUERTO RICO   SENEGAL
EL SALVADOR   JAMAICA   GAMBIA   UPPER
       NICARAGUA   GUINEA   VOLTA   NIGERIA
                                        SIERRA LEONE   IVORY
COSTA RICA   TRINIDAD AND TOBAGO   COAST GHANA
   PANAMA   VENEZUELA   LIBERIA   TOGO   CAMEROON
              GUYANA   BENIN
COLOMBIA   SURINAM   EQUATORIAL GUINEA
            FRENCH GUIANA   GABON
ECUADOR   CONGO

PERU   BRAZIL
                                                        AN

                                                        NAM
BOLIVIA

        PARAGUAY

                                        ● BAHRAIN
CHILE   URUGUAY
                                        ● FIJI
        ARGENTINA
                                        ● GRENADA

                                        ● MAURITIUS

                                        ● PUERTO RICO

                                        ● SINGAPORE

        FALKLAND ISLANDS   ● WESTERN SAMOA

UNION OF SOVIET SOCIALIST REPUBLICS

MONGOLIA

TURKEY

CYPRUS
LEBANON
SYRIA
ISRAEL
IRAQ
JORDAN
IRAN
KUWAIT
AFGHANISTAN

EGYPT

QATAR
U.A.E
OMAN

SAUDI ARABIA

N
YEMEN
S YEMEN

SUDAN

ETHIOPIA

SOMALIA

UGANDA
KENYA

TANZANIA

MALAWI

ZIMBABWE
whites
only

MOZAMBIQUE

MADAGASCAR

PAKISTAN

NEPAL
BHUTAN

INDIA

B
DESH
BURMA

SRI LANKA

CHINA

N
KOREA
S

JAPAN

TAIWAN

HONG KONG

LAOS

THAILAND
VIETNAM

KAM

PHILIPPINES

MALAYSIA
W

SINGAPORE

INDONESIA

PAPUA NEW
GUINEA

AUSTRALIA

NEW ZEALAND

Degree of trade union independence, early 1978

unions independent and comprise more than half the labour force

unions independent and comprise less than half the labour force

unions nominally independent but totally controlled

unions nominally independent but tightly controlled

unions nominally independent but severely repressed

virtually no recognised trade unionism

data not available

Source: Leading international trade union officials

Shares of world income and world population compared

Rich countries

20% world population
68% world income
= rich 'market economies'

9% world population
15% world income
= rich 'centrally-planned economies'

Poor countries

48% world population
12% world income
= poor 'market economies'

22% world population
5% world income
= Asian 'centrally-planned economies'

Incomes of the top 5% compared with the bottom 20% 1960s and early 1970s

- more than 30 times as much
- 21 — 30 times as much
- 11 — 20 times as much
- 6 — 10 times as much
- 1 — 5 times as much
- less than the bottom 20%
- data not available

Source: Shail Jain, Size Distribution of Income: a compilation of Data, World Bank 1975

GREENLAND

ICELAND

CANADA

NORWAY SWEDEN

DENMARK

IRELAND UNITED
KINGDOM
N E
W
B
V
GERMANY

CZECH
FRANCE AUST

SWITZERLAND

UNITED STATES OF AMERICA

SPAIN

PORTUGAL

ITALY

YUG

TUNISIA
1958

MEXICO

BAHAMAS

CUBA

JAMAICA

DOMINICAN REPUBLIC
PUERTO RICO

BELIZE
HONDURAS

HAITI
1954
1975-76

MOROCCO
1960

ALGERIA

LI

1962

GUATEMALA
EL SALVADOR

NICARAGUA
1972

BARBADOS

TRINIDAD AND TOBAGO

CAPE VERDE

MAURITANIA
1960
1971-74

MALI
1971-74

NIGER
1971-74

1951

COSTA RICA

PANAMA

VENEZUELA

GUYANA

SURINAM

SENEGAL
1971-74

GAMBIA
1973

1971-75
1977

GUINEA-BISSAU

UPPER
VOLTA

NIGERIA
1967-70
1971-74

COLOMBIA
1967

GUINEA

SIERRA LEONE

IVORY
COAST
1971-74
1977-78

BENIN

CAMEROON

LIBERIA

ECUADOR

1971-74

1971-74
1977
TOGO

GABON

CONGO

BRAZIL

PERU
1970

AN

BOLIVIA

NAM

PARAGUAY

CHILE
1960

URUGUAY

ARGENTINA

○ FIJI

○ HONG KONG

○ SINGAPORE

© Copyright Pluto Press

The Sahel drought
1973

MOROCCO

ALGERIA

LIBYA

EGYPT

MAURITANIA

MALI

NIGER

CHAD

SENEGAL

GAMBIA

GUINEA-BISSAU

GUINEA

UPPER
VOLTA

SUDAN

SIERRA LEONE

IVORY
COAST

GHANA

TOGO

BENIN

NIGERIA

CAR

LIBERIA

UNION OF SOVIET SOCIALIST REPUBLICS

MONGOLIA

N KOREA 1950-57
1959
S
JAPAN

TURKEY
1962
SYRIA IRAQ
LEBANON 1954
ISRAEL
GYPT
1974
SAUDI ARABIA

AFGHANISTAN
1971-72
IRAN
PAKISTAN
1950-58
1960
1971-73

QATAR
U A E
OMAN

NEPAL
INDIA
1950-55
1965-67
1972

B-
DESH
1970-75

BURMA

CHINA

TAIWAN
1959
HONG KONG

SUDAN
1973
N
YEMEN
S YEMEN
DJIBOUTI
ETHIOPIA
1973-79
SOMALIA
1974-75
UGANDA
KENYA
1976
RE
72
TANZANIA

SRI LANKA

LAOS
THAILAND
VIETNAM
1954
1961
1964
1968
1975
KAM
1970
1975-76 1978-9

PHILIPPINES
1972

BRUNEI
MALAYSIA

1979 MALAWI
IA
MBABWE MOZAMBIQUE
1971-74

MADAGASCAR

1974

INDONESIA
1977

PAPUA
NEW GUINEA
1975-79

AUSTRALIA

Food and famines

Calories available per head
as a proportion of estimated requirement
1972-74

below requirement:

over 20% below

10.1 — 20% below

0.1 — 10% below

above requirement:

0.1 — 10% above

10.1 — 20% above

20.1 — 30% above

over 30% above

data not available

Extreme range: Upper Volta 27% below requirement —
Czechoslovakia, Ireland, Portugal 41% above requirement

Countries with major famines 1950-79

NEW ZEALAND

Source: FAO Fourth World Food Survey, 1977 Science, 9 May 1975, and the press

GREENLAND

NORWAY
68 75

72 78

ICELAND
73 79   68 74   72 7
                                    SWEDE
UNITED KINGDOM   72 7
                                    DENMARK
IRELAND   W E
69 74   68 74   GERMANY   PO
                                    CZECH
                              B   AUS
                        70 77 S
                        FRANCE ITALY Y
                   65 72   70 75   69 75
                   PORTUGAL SPAIN
CANADA   53 56
69 76   51 55 TUNISIA
                              52 55   51 55 LI
UNITED STATES OF AMERICA   MOROCCO
69 77
                                    ALGERIA

                        CAPE   39 42   37 40
         69 72 CUBA BAHAMAS VERDE   37 40 MALI 37 40
MEXICO   DOMINICAN REPUBLIC 39 42 SENEGAL MAURITANIA 29
63 67   63 67 HAITI   57 59   GAMBIA 32 31   NIGER CH
         52 55 JAMAICA PUERTO RICO   GUINEA-BISSAU U.VOLTA 37 37
48 50 GUATEMALA   69 76   39 42 GUINEA BENIN NIGERIA
EL SALVADOR 51 55   BARBADOS   SIERRA LEONE 42 45 IVORY TOGO 39 43 CAM
57 60 NICARAGUA   59 63   42 45 LIBERIA COAST 42 45
         COSTA RICA 63 67 GUYANA   46 44 GHANA 32 39   GABON
66 70 PANAMA 59 63 SURINAM   42 45   CONGO
         COLOMBIA FR GUYANA   39 43 ANG
65 67   25 45

         ECUADOR   42 45   39
54 58
                                                  NAMIBIA

ALBANIA   PERU
65 67   53 55   BRAZIL
                          58 61
AUSTRIA
68 75   BOLIVIA
HAITI   46 48
49 51
                 60 64
HONG KONG   PAR
67 75

HUNGARY   Infant mortality   Life expectancy
67 72   Deaths in first year of life
                 Europe and N. America 1976-77   52 55
LUXEMBOURG   others 1970-75
67 74   CHILE   Hospital beds per
         65 72 URUGUAY   below 20   100,000 population
SWITZERLAND   ARGENTINA   where data available
70 76   60 66   65 71   20 - 50   over 600

TRINIDAD AND TOBAGO   51-100
64 68
                                  101-150   401 — 600
YUGOSLAVIA
65 70   151-200   201 — 400

                                  over 200   200 and below

                                  data not available

Source: UN Statistical Yearbook 1978, UN Demographic Yearbook 1977

ICELAND

NORWAY

SWEDEN

IRELAND

DENMARK

UNITED KINGDOM

EAST GERMANY POLAND

CZECH

WEST AUSTRIA HUNGARY

PORTUGAL

FRANCE

SWITZ

ITALY YUGO

SPAIN

ALB

GREECE

CANADA

Primary & Secondary 87%

UNITED STATES OF AMERICA

MEXICO

BAHAMAS

TUNISIA

LIBYA

CUBA

DOMINICAN REPUBLIC

MOROCCO

ALGERIA

GUATEMALA

JAMAICA

HAITI

PUERTO RICO

EL SALVADOR

BARBADOS

MAURITANIA

MALI

NIGER

HONDURAS

TRIN

GAMBIA

SENEGAL

VOLTA

NICARAGUA

VENEZUELA

GUYANA

GUINEA

IVORY
COAST

GHANA

BENIN

NIGERIA

COSTA RICA

SURINAM

GUINEA-BISSAU

CAMEROON

PANAMA

COLOMBIA

GABON

ECUADOR

CONGO

ALBANIA

SIERRA LEONE

LIBERIA

AUSTRIA

PERU

BRAZIL

BELGIUM

EQUATORIAL GUINEA

AN

BULGARIA

NETHERLANDS

NAM

BURUNDI

ROMANIA

BOLIVIA

PARAGUAY

CZECHOSLOVAKIA

RWANDA

EAST GERMANY

SINGAPORE

ARGENTINA

Literacy

LUXEMBOURG

SWITZERLAND

URUGUAY

Adult illiterates as a proportion of
the population 15 years old and over

MALTA

UPPER VOLTA

CHILE

over 80%

61 – 80%

MAURITIUS

ZIMBABWE

FALKLAND ISLANDS

41 – 60%

21 – 40%

20% and below

data not available

Extreme range: Niger 98.6% — USSR 0.3%

UNION OF SOVIET SOCIALIST REPUBLICS

Education

Primary school enrolment
as proportion of population 6—11 years old

50% and below   50.1 — 90%   over 90%
Extreme range: Gabon 202% — Bhutan 12%

Secondary school enrolment
as proportion of population 12—18 years old

25% and below   25.2—50%   over 50%
Extreme range: Finland 97% — Bhutan 1%

Enrolment in tertiary level education
as proportion of population 20—24 years old

5% and below   5.1—20%   over 20%

Extreme range: USA 57.64% — for example,
Equatorial Guinea, Gambia, Mauritania,
Bhutan, with none

Source: UNESCO Statistical Yearbook 1977

GREENLAND

NETHERLANDS
BELGIUM
ICELAND
NORWAY
SWE
DENMARK
IRELAND
UNITED
KINGDOM
W. PE
GERMANY
CANADA
LUXEMBOURG
FRANCE
PORTUGAL
SPAIN
SWITZERLAND
ITALY

UNITED STATES OF AMERICA
TUNISIA

MOROCCO
ALGERIA
LIBYA

MEXICO
BAHAMAS

CUBA
JAMAICA
DOMINICAN REPUBLIC
BELIZE
HAITI
PUERTO RICO
GUATEMALA
HONDURAS
EL SALVADOR
NICARAGUA
COSTA RICA
BARBADOS
PANAMA
TRINIDAD AND TOBAGO

MAURITANIA
MALI
NIGER

GAMBIA
SENEGAL
GUINEA-BISSAU
GUINEA
UPPER
VOLTA
SIERRA LEONE
NIGERIA
IVORY
COAST
BENIN
LIBERIA
TOGO
EQUATORIAL GUINEA

VENEZUELA
GUYANA
SURINAM
COLOMBIA

ECUADOR
CAMEROON

PERU
GABON
CONGO

BRAZIL

BOLIVIA

AN

CHILE
PARAGUAY
NAM

URUGUAY
ARGENTINA

FIJI

HONG KONG

MAURITIUS

WESTERN SAMOA

**Newsprint consumption
per head in 1977**

	above 15 kilogrammes
	10.1—15 kilogrammes
	5.1—10 kilogrammes
	1.1—5 kilogrammes
	1 kilogramme and below
	data not available

Source UN Statistical Yearbook 1978

UNION OF SOVIET SOCIALIST REPUBLICS

FINLAND

MONGOLIA

CHINA

N. KOREA

S. KOREA

JAPAN

GARIA

TURKEY

CYPRUS

SYRIA

ISRAEL

IRAQ

JORDAN

AFGHANISTAN

IRAN

KUWAIT

QATAR

SAUDI ARABIA

UNITED ARAB EMIRATES

GYPT

PAKISTAN

YEMEN

OMAN

N. YEMEN

NEPAL

BHUTAN

BANGLADESH

INDIA

BURMA

LAOS

THAILAND

KAM

VIETNAM

HONG KONG

TAIWAN

PHILIPPINES

SRI LANKA

MALAYSIA

BRUNEI

SINGAPORE

INDONESIA

PAPUA NEW GUINEA

UDAN

ETHIOPIA

SOMALIA

KENYA

TANZANIA

MALAWI

MADAGASCAR

MOZAMBIQUE

BABWE

MAURITIUS

AUSTRALIA

Telephones per 1000 population in 1976

Where data available

over 500

401—500

301—400

201—300

101—200

11—101

10 and below

AUSTRIA

BAHRAIN

FIJI

WESTERN SAMOA

Source UN Statistical Yearbook 1978

NEW ZEALAND

MAURITIUS

Welfare receipts as a proportion of GDP
1974 or most recent year

	2% and below		10.1 — 15%
	2.1 — 5%		above 15%
	5.1 — 10%		data not available

Extreme range: Singapore 0.44% — Sweden 20.74%

Source: ILO

© Copyright Pluto Press

Growth in urban population
1950-75

over 400%

301 — 400%

201 — 300%

101 — 200%

51 — 100%

50% and below

urban decline

data not available

Extreme range: N. and S. Yemen
688% growth — East Germany 1.5% decline

decline in rural population

Source: UN, World Population Trends and Policies, 1977.
Monitoring Report Vol. 1, 1979

UNION OF SOVIET SOCIALIST REPUBLICS

MONGOLIA

KOREA

JAPAN

TURKEY

CYPRUS

SYRIA

LEB

ISRAEL

IRAQ

IRAN

AFGHANISTAN

CHINA

JORDAN

KUWAIT

PAKISTAN

EGYPT

QATAR

U.A.E.

OMAN

SAUDI ARABIA

NEPAL

TAIWAN

HONG KONG

INDIA

BURMA

N YEMEN

S YEMEN

BH

DESH

LAOS

SUDAN

THAILAND

ETHIOPIA

VIETNAM

KAM

PHILIPPINES

SOMALIA

SRI LANKA

UGANDA

KENYA

MALAYSIA

TANZANIA

INDONESIA

PAPUA NEW GUINEA

MALAWI

MADAGASCAR

MBABWE

MOZAMBIQUE

S

AUSTRALIA

NEW ZEALAND

Housing and urban slums

Proportion of population without a safe water supply in 1976

- 20% and below
- 21 - 40%
- 41 - 60%
- 61 - 80%
- over 80%
- data not available

Extreme range: Bahrain, Denmark, Iceland, Israel, Sweden and UK 1% – Gabon 99%

Proportion of city populations in slum and squatter settlements late 1960s and early 1970s

- 20% and below
- 21 - 40%
- 41 - 60%
- 61 - 80%
- over 80%

Source: R.L. Sivard, World Military and Social Expenditures 1979.
UN, World Housing Survey 1974

CANADA

UNITED STATES OF AMERICA

MEXICO

BAHAMAS

CUBA
HAITI DOMINICAN REPUBLIC
JAMAICA PUERTO RICO

GUATEMALA HONDURAS
EL SALVADOR
NICARAGUA
COSTA RICA
PANAMA

BARBADOS
TRINIDAD AND TOBAGO

VENEZUELA
SURINAM GUYANA

COLOMBIA

ECUADOR

PERU

BRAZIL

BOLIVIA

PARAGUAY

CHILE

URUGUAY

ARGENTINA

ICELAND

NETHERLANDS

LUXEMBOURG

NORWAY SWEDEN FIN

DENMARK

IRELAND

UNITED
KINGDOM
BELGIUM GERMANY
WEST EAST POLAND

CZECHOSLOVAKIA

FRANCE SWITZ AUSTRIA
HUNGARY

YUGOSLAVIA

PORTUGAL

SPAIN ITALY ALBANIA
GR

TUNISIA

MOROCCO ALGERIA

LIB

MAURITANIA
MALI NIGER

SENEGAL
GAMBIA UPPER
GUINEA VOLTA BEN
IN
SIERRA LEONE
LIBERIA IVORY NIGERIA
CO-ST

CAMEROON
EQUATORIAL
GHANA GUINEA

GABON
CONGO

AN

NAM

Legend (symbols with bars):

- BAHRAIN
- FIJI
- MALTA
- MAURITIUS
- MONACO
- NETHERLANDS ANTILLES
- ST. KITTS-NEVIS-ANGUILLA
- SINGAPORE
- SOLOMON ISLANDS

Murder

Murders recorded for every 100,000 population
Annual average 1973-76 or nearest equivalent

- 2 and below
- 2.1 - 5
- 5.1 - 10
- 10.1 - 15
- above 15
- data not available

Extreme range: Bahrain .2 - Nigeria 40.7

Source: Interpol, International Crime Statistics
US Dept. of Commerce, Bureau of the Census,
Statistical Abstract of the United States.

UNION OF SOVIET SOCIALIST REPUBLICS

MONGOLIA

CHINA

N KOREA

S KOREA

JAPAN

TAIWAN

IRAN

AFGHANISTAN

PAKISTAN

NEPAL

BHU

INDIA

BANGLADESH

BURMA

LAOS

HONG KONG

THAILAND

KAMPU CHEA

S VIETNAM

PHILIPPINES

SRI LANKA

MALAYSIA

SINGAPORE

INDONESIA

PAPUA NEW GUINEA

AUSTRALIA

NEW ZEALAND

KEY *inset*

PRUS

SYRIA

ISRAEL

IRAQ

KUWAIT

QATAR

U.A.E

OMAN

SAUDI ARABIA

S YEMEN

N Y

YPT

DAN

ETHIOPIA

SOMALIA

DA

KENYA

TANZANIA

MALAWI

BIA

MADAGASCAR

ABWE

MOZAMBIQUE

S

inset

TURKEY

CYPRUS

LEBANON

ISRAEL

SYRIA

IRAQ

JORDAN

SAUDI ARABIA

Crime

Crimes recorded (other than traffic offences)
for every **100,000** population

Annual average **1973-76** or nearest equivalent
Where data available

1000 and under	1001 -3000	3001 -5000	above 5000

Extreme range: Philippines 81 — Lebanon 34,791

Unemployment throughout the world is
enormous and growing. This is admitted
everywhere, but official statistics tend to
disguise rather than reveal the extent. For this
reason it has been impossible to produce a
useful map on the problem. Instead this
diagram shows a projected growth in world
population and its division into employed
labour force and inactive population, 1750-2150

year

2150

2100

2050

2000

**Projected growth in world population
and division into
employed labour force and inactive population**

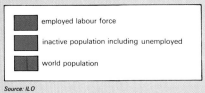

employed labour force

inactive population including unemployed

world population

Source: ILO

people

11000 million   10000 million   9000 million   8000 million   7000 million   6000 million   5000 million

South Asia
East Asia
Africa
Latin America

Europe
USSR
North America
Oceania

year

2150

2100

2050

2000

1970 | 1970

1900 | 1900

1850 | 1850

1800 | 1800

1750 | 1750

million | 3000 million | 2000 million | 1000 million | 0 | 0 | 1000 million | 2000 million

people

CANADA

Thule

GREENLAND

Kap Tobin

ICELAND

★ Helena

★ Moosonee

★ Salt Lake City

★ Richmond   ★ Rocky Flats

★ New York

UNITED STATES OF AMERICA

Miami

MEXICO

CUBA   BAHAMAS

JAMAICA

DOMINICAN REPUBLIC

BELIZE
HONDURAS   HAITI

GUATEMALA
EL SALVADOR

NICARAGUA   ● BARBADOS

COSTA RICA   ★ Balboa   TRINIDAD AND TOBAGO

PANAMA   VENEZUELA

GUYANA
SURINAM

COLOMBIA

ECUADOR

Guayaquil ★

PERU   BRAZIL

★ Lima

BOLIVIA

PARAGUAY

CHILE

URUGUAY

ARGENTINA

FALKLAND
ISLANDS

IRELAND   UNITED
KINGDO

London

FRA

PORTUGAL   SPAIN

★ Madrid

TUNISIA

MOROCCO   ALGERIA   LI

MAURITANIA   MALI   NIGER

SENEGAL
GAMBIA

GUINEA-BISSAU   GUINEA   UPPER
VOLTA   BENIN   NIGERIA

SIERRA LEONE   IVORY
COAST   GHANA   TOGO   CAMEROON

LIBERIA   EQUATORIAL GUINEA

GABON
CONGO

AN

NAM

Lead pollution
One example in the Western Hemisphere

● 10 femtocuries per cubic metre

Source: US Energy Research and Development
Association, Health and Safety Laboratory

Principal areas of damage to the sea

pollution

Source: Earthscan

Sulphuric acid/sulphur dioxide pollution
Two examples: Europe and Japan

100 micrograms per cubic metre

Source: World Health Organization, Global Environmental Monitoring System 1976

RWAY
DENMARK
SWEDEN
Copenhagen
WEST GERMANY
EAST GERMANY
POLAND
Frankfurt
Prague
CZECH
AUSTRIA
HUNGARY
ROMANIA
ITALY
Zagreb
YUGOSLAVIA
BULG
ALBANIA
Rome
GREECE

UNION OF SOVIET SOCIALIST REPUBLICS

MONGOLIA

TURKEY
SYRIA
IRAQ
IRAN
AFGHANISTAN
CHINA
N KOREA
S
JAPAN
Tokyo
PAKISTAN
NEPAL
BHUTAN
EGYPT
SAUDI ARABIA
UNITED ARAB EMIRATES
OMAN
N YEMEN
S YEMEN
INDIA
B-DESH
BURMA
LA
TAIWAN
THAILAND
KAM
VIETNAM
PHILIPPINES
UDAN
ETHIOPIA
SOMALIA
SRI LANKA
MALAYSIA
UGANDA
KENYA
TANZANIA
INDONESIA
PAPUA NEW GUINEA
BIA
MADAGASCAR
MOZAMBIQUE
BABWE

AUSTRALIA

NEW ZEALAND

Pollution in the Mediterranean

★ focal points

■ tar (10 milligrams per square metre)

▨ sewage and fertilizer (100,000 tons per year)

FRANCE
Marseilles
Venice
Genoa
Livorno
Rome
ROMANIA
YUGOSLAVIA
BULGARIA
Istanbul
SPAIN
CORSICA
Naples
ALBANIA
Salonika
TURKEY
Valencia
SARDINIA
GREECE
Izmir
Alicante
BALEARIC ISLANDS
Athens
CYPRUS
Malaga
SICILY
LEBANON
SYRIA
JORDAN
Algiers
MALTA
CRETE
ISRAEL
OROCCO
ALGERIA
TUNISIA
LIBYA
Alexandria
EGYPT

urce: UN Evironmental Program 1977

GREENLAND

ICELAND

CANADA

UNITED STATES
OF AMERICA

MEXICO

BAHAMAS

CUBA
JAMAICA
HAITI
DOMINICAN REPUBLIC
PUERTO RICO
BELIZE
GUATEMALA
HONDURAS
EL SALVADOR
COSTA RICA
PANAMA

BARBADOS
TRINIDAD AND TOBAGO

VENEZUELA
GUYANA
SURINAM
COLOMBIA
ECUADOR
PERU
BRAZIL
BOLIVIA
PARAGUAY
CHILE
ARGENTINA
URUGUAY

FALKLAND ISLANDS

NORWAY
SWEDEN
UNITED DENMARK
KINGDOM
IRELAND
NETH W E
GERMANY
BEL
LUX
CZEC
AUS
FRANCE
SWI
ITALY

PORTUGAL
SPAIN
TUNISIA

MOROCCO
ALGERIA
LI

MAURITANIA
MALI
NIGER

SENEGAL
GAMBIA
GUINEA-BISSAU
GUINEA
UPPER
VOLTA
SIERRA LEONE
IVORY
COAST
GHANA
BENIN
NIGERIA
LIBERIA
TOGO
CAMEROON
EQUATORIAL GUINEA
GABON
CONGO

AN

NAM

'More than one third of the earth's land
is arid. Much of it has become desert since
the dawn of civilization, and many vulnerable
areas are even now being turned into desert.
This process has intensified in recent decades,
and threatens the future of 628 million people
or that 14 per cent of the world's population
who live in the drylands; of this number,
between 50 and 78 million people are affected
directly by decreases in productivity associated
with current desertification processes.
In the past half century, on the southern edge of
the Sahara alone, as much as 650,000 sq. km of
once productive land has become desert.'

Report of UN Conference on Desertification,1977

Source: UN World Map of Desertification 1977

© *Copyright Pluto Press*

The Sands of Negligence

Bioclimatic zones

	hyper-arid
	arid
	semi-arid
	sub-humid
	humid

Areas of risk

	very high
	moderate
	highly vulnerable land
	high human/mechanical pressure
	high animal pressure

54. The Dying Earth

UNION OF SOVIET SOCIALIST REPUBLICS

MONGOLIA

N KOREA

S KOREA

JAPAN

CHINA

TAIWAN

KEY

PRUS

SYRIA

IRAQ

IRAN

AFGHANISTAN

KUWAIT

QATAR

U.A.E

OMAN

PAKISTAN

NEPAL

BHUTAN

BAN.

INDIA

BURMA

LAOS

THAILAND

KAMP

VIETNAM

GYPT

JDAN

SAUDI
ARABIA

N
YEMEN

YEMEN

SRI LANKA

PHILIPPINES

ETHIOPIA

SOMALIA

MALAYSIA

W

UGANDA

KENYA

B

INDONESIA

TANZANIA

MALAWI

MADAGASCAR

PAPUA
NEW
GUINEA

IA

BABWE

MOZAMBIQUE

AUSTRALIA

Murdered Land

War pollution in Vietnam, Kampuchea and Laos 1965-70

NORTH VIETNAM

7.1%

Hue

10.3%

LAOS

10.2%

Military Region 1

100.1%

4.7% Pleiku

23.2%

KAMPUCHEA

R. Mekong

SOUTH
VIETNAM

4.4%

23.7% Military Region 2

Phnom Penh

30%

Saigon
Military Region 3

4%

South China Sea

11.6%

Military Region 4

proportion of surface area
of each military region

bombarded with flying
'shrapnel' or metal shards

sprayed with herbicides

NEW ZEALAND

ICELAND

NORWAY

SWEDEN

FINLAND

IRELAND

UNITED KINGDOM

DENMARK

NETH

BEL

LUX

WEST GERMANY

EAST

POLAND

CZECHOSLOVAKIA

FRANCE

SWITZ

AUSTRIA

HUNGARY

PORTUGAL

SPAIN

ITALY

YUGOSLAVIA

ALB

GREECE

CANADA

UNITED STATES OF AMERICA

MEXICO

BAHAMAS

CUBA

JAMAICA

HAITI

DOMINICAN REPUBLIC

PUERTO RICO

GUATEMALA

EL SALVADOR

HONDURAS

NICARAGUA

COSTA RICA

PANAMA

BARBADOS

TRINIDAD AND TOBAGO

VENEZUELA

GUYANA

SURINAM

FRENCH GUIANA

COLOMBIA

ECUADOR

BRAZIL

PERU

BOLIVIA

PARAGUAY

CHILE

URUGUAY

ARGENTINA

TUNISIA

MOROCCO

ALGERIA

LI

MAURITANIA

MALI

NIGER

SENEGAL

GAMBIA

UPPER VOLTA

GUINEA-BISSAU

GUINEA

NIGERIA

SIERRA LEONE

IVORY COAST

GHANA

BENIN

TOGO

LIBERIA

EQUATORIAL GUINEA

CAMEROON

GABON

CONGO

AN

NAM

© Copyright Pluto Press

UNION OF SOVIET SOCIALIST REPUBLICS

MONGOLIA

CHINA

TURKEY

CYPRUS
LEBANON
ISRAEL
SYRIA
IRAQ
AFGHANISTAN

N KOREA
S
JAPAN

IRAN

EGYPT

KUWAIT

QATAR

U.A.E.

SAUDI ARABIA

PAKISTAN

NEPAL

BHUTAN

TAIWAN

OMAN

N
YEMEN
S
YEMEN

INDIA

B-
DESH

BURMA

LAOS

PHILIPPINES

SUDAN

THAILAND

VIETNAM

KAM

ETHIOPIA

SOMALIA

SRI LANKA

KENYA

UGANDA

MALAYSIA

TANZANIA

MALAWI

MADAGASCAR

INDONESIA

PAPUA
NEW GUINEA

BABWE

MOZAMBIQUE

AUSTRALIA

Changes in industrial growth

Average annual increase/decrease in industrial growth rate between 1960-70 and 1970-78

Increase in growth rate:

  over 50%

  25 — 50%

  up to 25%

Decrease in growth rate:

  up to 25%

  25 — 50%

  over 50%

  data not available

  manufacturing only

Extreme range: Morocco 86.9% increase
— Mozambique, Chile, Venezuela: absolute decline in 1970-78

Source: UN Monthly Bulletin of Statistics, November 1979
UN Statistical Yearbook, 1978

NEW ZEALAND

GREENLAND

ICELAND

FAROE ISLANDS

CANADA

NORWAY

SWEDEN

DENMARK

IRELAND

UNITED KINGDOM

N

W GERMANY

P

E

CZE

AUS

UNITED STATES OF AMERICA

FRANCE

ITALY

PORTUGAL

SPAIN

TUNISIA

MOROCCO

ALGERIA

LIB

MEXICO

BAHAMAS

CUBA

HAITI

DOMINICAN REPUBLIC

BELIZE

JAMAICA

HONDURAS

PUERTO RICO

GUATEMALA

EL SALVADOR

NICARAGUA

MAURITANIA

MALI

NIGER

CAPE VERDE

SENEGAL

C

GAMBIA

UPPER VOLTA

NIGERIA

BARBADOS

GUINEA-BISSAU

COSTA RICA

PANAMA

TRINIDAD AND TOBAGO

GUINEA

SIERRA LEONE

IVORY COAST

GHANA

BENIN

TOGO

VENEZUELA

GUYANA

SURINAM

LIBERIA

CAMEROON

EQUATORIAL GUINEA

C

COLOMBIA

GABON

ECUADOR

CONGO

PERU

BRAZIL

ANG

BOLIVIA

NAM

PARAGUAY

CHILE

URUGUAY

ARGENTINA

BAHRAIN

MAURITIUS

FALKLAND ISLANDS

SINGAPORE

Annual inflation rates, 1974

- over 50%
- 25.1 — 50%
- 20.1 — 25%
- 15.1 — 20%
- 10.1 — 15%
- 5.1 — 10%
- below 5%
- data not available

Extreme range: Chile 585.9%
— Niger 3.6%

Source: IMF Industrial Financial Statistics,
April 1977

CANADA

UNITED STATES OF AMERICA

MEXICO

BAHAMAS

CUBA

JAMAICA   HAITI   DOMINICAN REPUBLIC
PUERTO RICO

GUATEMALA   HONDURAS
EL SALVADOR
NICARAGUA
COSTA RICA   PANAMA

GRENADA   BARBADOS
TRINIDAD AND TOBAGO

VENEZUELA
GUYANA
SURINAM

COLOMBIA

ECUADOR

PERU

BRAZIL

BOLIVIA

PARAGUAY

URUGUAY

CHILE

ARGENTINA

ICELAND

NORWAY   SWEDEN

DENMARK

IRELAND   UNITED
KINGDOM
GERMANY
W   E
N
B
S
CZEC
FRANCE   AUST
ITALY

PORTUGAL   SPAIN

TUNISIA

MOROCCO   ALGERIA   LI

MAURITANIA

CAPE VERDE

SENEGAL
GAMBIA

MALI   NIGER

UPPER
VOLTA
GUINEA
BENIN
SIERRA LEONE   IVORY
COAST   GHANA   NIGERIA
LIBERIA   TOGO
CAMEROON
EQUATORIAL GUINEA

GABON
CONGO

AN

NAM

FIJI

MALTA

MAURITIUS

Growth in the money supply
Annual average 1968-77

over 100%

50.1 – 100%

40.1 – 50%

30.1 – 40%

20.1 – 30%

10.1 – 20%

10% and below

data not available

Extreme range:
Chile 36,118% – Bahamas 0.17%

Source: UN Statistical Yearbook 1978

UNION OF SOVIET SOCIALIST REPUBLICS

MONGOLIA

CHINA

N. KOREA
S.

JAPAN

TURKEY
CYPRUS
LEBANON
SYRIA
ISRAEL
IRAQ
JORDAN
IRAN
AFGHANISTAN
KUWAIT
BAHRAIN
QATAR
U.A.E.
OMAN
SAUDI ARABIA
PAKISTAN
NEPAL
BHUTAN
GYPT
SUDAN
N
YEMEN
S
YEMEN
INDIA
B-
DESH
BURMA
TAIWAN
HONG KONG
ETHIOPIA
SOMALIA
THAILAND
VIETNAM
LAOS
KAM
PHILIPPINES
SRI LANKA
UGANDA
KENYA
DA
NDI
TANZANIA
MALAWI
MALAYSIA
SINGAPORE
IA
RBABWE
MADAGASCAR
MOZAMBIQUE
INDONESIA
PAPUA
NEW GUINEA
AUSTRALIA

**Decline in purchasing power
of national currencies 1950-75**

	above 90%		51 — 60%
	81 — 90%		50% and below
	71 — 80%		data not available
	61 — 70%		

Source: Pick's Currency Yearbook
1976-77

Destruction of paper money

NEW
ZEALAND

CANADA

UNITED STATES OF AMERICA

Other N. Atlantic countries
including transnationals 318.4%
International institutions 323%

MEXICO

BAHAMAS

CUBA

JAMAICA HAITI DOMINICAN REPUBLIC
PUERTO RICO

GUATEMALA HONDURAS
EL SALVADOR

NICARAGUA

COSTA RICA BARBADOS
PANAMA TRINIDAD AND TOBAGO

VENEZUELA GUYANA
SURINAM

COLOMBIA

ECUADOR

Other 'developing countries'
(non-OPEC) 375%

PERU

BRAZIL

BOLIVIA

CHILE PARAGUAY

URUGUAY

ARGENTINA

ICELAND

NORWAY SWEDEN
DENMARK

IRELAND UNITED N GERMANY P
KINGDOM W   E
B CZECH

FRANCE S AUST
YUGO

PORTUGAL SPAIN ITALY

MOROCCO TUNISIA

ALGERIA LIB

Other 'developing countries'
(OPEC) 267%

MAURITANIA MALI NIGER

SENEGAL UPPER CH
GAMBIA VOLTA
GUINEA-BISSAU GUINEA

Euro-currencies

Growth/decline in publicly-announced
Euro-currency bank credits between 1975 and 1979

Growth

more than 1000%

501 — 1000%

251 — 500%

250% and below

Decline

1979 less than 1975

data not available

Extreme range: Venezuela 19,137 % increase
— Japan, Iran 100% decrease

Source: Morgan Guaranty Trust, World Financial
Markets, May 1978 and January 1980

CANADA
15%

UNITED STATES OF AMERICA
15.25%

IRELAND
15.5%

MEXICO
19%

BAHAMAS

CUBA HAITI DOMINICAN REPUBLIC
JAMAICA PUERTO RICO

GUATEMALA HONDURAS
EL SALVADOR

NICARAGUA BARBADOS
TRINIDAD AND TOBAGO

COSTA RICA VENEZUELA GUYANA
PANAMA 13% SURINAM

COLOMBIA

ECUADOR

PERU

BRAZIL
61.82%

BOLIVIA

CHILE PARAGUAY

URUGUAY

ARGENTINA

SF

FALKLAND ISLANDS

Source: Morgan Guaranty Trust, World Financial
Markets, November 1978 and January 1980

UNION OF SOVIET SOCIALIST REPUBLICS

*Other 'centrally-planned economies'
including COMECON institutions 242.7%
(increase mainly due to China's entry as a borrower in 1979)*

MONGOLIA

TURKEY

CYPRUS
LEBANON
ISRAEL
SYRIA
IRAQ
IRAN
AFGHANISTAN
CHINA
N KOREA
S KOREA
JAPAN

EGYPT
KUWAIT
QATAR
U A E
OMAN
SAUDI ARABIA
PAKISTAN
NEPAL
BHU
INDIA
B DESH
BURMA
TAIWAN
HONG KONG

SUDAN
N YEMEN
S YEMEN
ETHIOPIA
LAOS
THAILAND
VIETNAM
KAM
PHILIPPINES

MALAYSIA

INDONESIA
PAPUA NEW GUINEA

AUSTRALIA

NEW ZEALAND

The inset (lower left) — Europe:

NORWAY 11%
7.85% FINLAND
SWEDEN 13.75%
DENMARK 13.75%
NETHER-LANDS 15%
GERMANY
WEST
EAST
UNION OF SOVIET SOCIALIST REPUBLICS
POLAND
BELG 15.25%
9.75%
CZECHOSLOVAKIA
FRANCE 13.65%
5% SWITZ
AUSTRIA
HUNGARY
ROMANIA
19.5% ITALY
YUGOSLAVIA
BULGARIA

The inset (lower middle) — Asia:

CHINA
N KOREA
S KOREA 18.5%
6.31% JAPAN
TAIWAN
14.5% HONG KONG
VIETNAM
KAM
THAILAND
SINGAPORE 9.5%
MALAYSIA
PHILIPPINES 16%
INDONESIA
PAPUA NEW GUINEA

AUSTRALIA 10.75%

NEW ZEALAND 12%

Africa (lower left):

ZAIRE
TANZANIA
ANGOLA
ZAMBIA
MALAWI
ZIM
NAMIBIA
BOTS
MOZAM BIQUE
9.5%
MADAGASCAR
SOUTH AFRICA

The Rising Cost of Money

**Growth/decline in bank lending rates
to prime borrowers between 1975 and 1979**

Growth	Decline
over 100%	0 – 25%
75.1 – 100%	over 25%
50.1 – 75%	data not available
25.1 – 50%	
0 – 25%	

Hong Kong

Singapore

*Figures on countries show
best lending rates of banks,
December 1979*

inset

CYPRUS
SYRIA
LEBANON
ISRAEL
IRAQ
JORDAN
SAUDI ARABIA

UNION OF SOVIET SOCIALIST REPUBLICS

0.1

5.59

MONGOLIA

.7

TURKEY
inset
SYRIA
LEBANON
ISRAEL
IRAQ
IRAN
AFGHANISTAN
KUWAIT
BAHRAIN
QATAR
U.A.E.
OMAN
SAUDI ARABIA
PAKISTAN
NEPAL
BHUTAN
CHINA

N KOREA
S
JAPAN
0.1

TAIWAN
HONG KONG

0.87

GYPT
N S
YEMEN YEMEN

0.32

UDAN
ETHIOPIA
SOMALIA
UGANDA
KENYA
B
TANZANIA
MBIA
MALAWI
MADAGASCAR
BABWE
MOZAMBIQUE
S

INDIA

B-
DESH
BURMA
Burma Laos
Vietnam combined
THAILAND
KAM
VIETNAM

PHILIPPINES

SRI LANKA

MALAYSIA
SINGAPORE
W

INDONESIA

PAPUA
NEW GUINEA

Growth/decline in relative value between 1970 and 1979

Growth

over 25% growth

0 – 25% growth

Decline

0 – 25% decline

over 25% decline

Extreme range: Switzerland 89.8% growth — Italy 50.9% decline

Source: Morgan Guaranty Trust, World Financial Markets, January 1980

The Major Currencies

AUSTRALIA

NEW ZEALAND

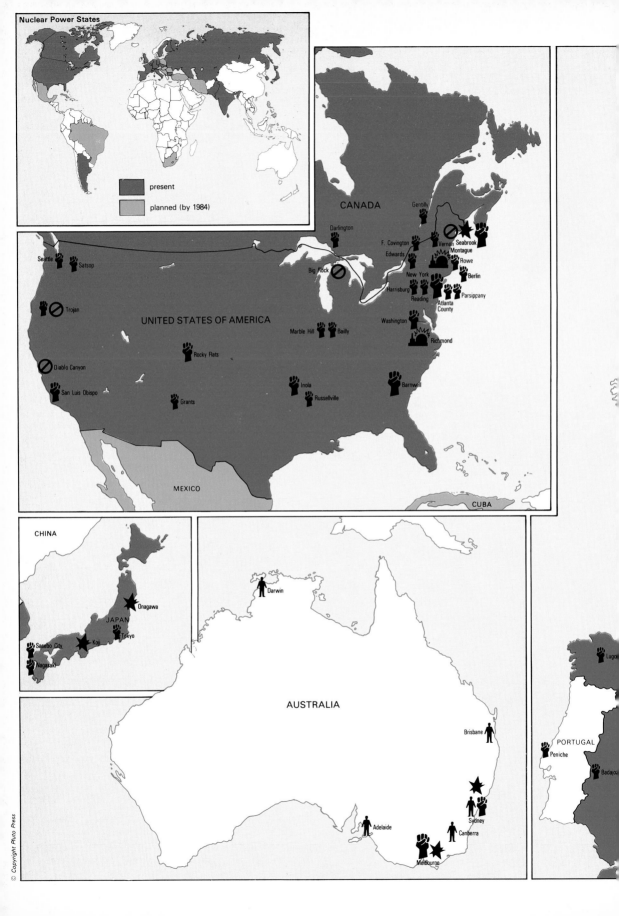

Nuclear Power States

present

planned (by 1984)

CANADA

Gentilly

Darlington

F. Covington
Edwards
Big Rock
Vernon Seabrook
Montague
Rowe
Berlin

New York
Harrisburg
Reading
Parsippany
Atlanta
County
Washington
Richmond

Seattle Satsop

Trojan

UNITED STATES OF AMERICA

Diablo Canyon

San Luis Obispo

Rocky Flats

Marble Hill Bailly

Grants

Inola
Russellville

Barnwell

MEXICO

CUBA

CHINA

Onagawa

JAPAN
Tokyo

Sasebo City Koji

Nagasaki

Darwin

AUSTRALIA

Brisbane

Adelaide

Sydney

Canberra

Melbourne

PORTUGAL
Peniche

Lugo

Badajoz

© Copyright Pluto Press

FINLAND

NORWAY

SWEDEN

UNION OF SOVIET
SOCIALIST REPUBLICS

Helsinki

Orkney Is

Stockholm

Torness

Glasgow   Edinburgh

Loch Doon

Barrow   Windscale   Hartlepool

Eysham

Liverpool

Capenhurst

UNITED KINGDOM

Goteborg

DENMARK

Gyllingnaes

Barsebaeck

Hojstrup

Brokdorf

Gassette   Esenshamm   Gorleben

POLAND

Almelo   Hanover

NETHERLANDS

Borssele   Gronau

Kalkar   Grohnde

EAST
GERMANY

London

Dungeness

La Hague   Gravelines   BELGIUM

Cherbourg   Dieppe   Aachen   Bonn

Flammanville

WEST GERMANY

CZECHOSLOVAKIA

Brennilis

Plogoff

Paris

Nogent-sur-Seine

Thionville

Whyl   Kaiseraugst

Zwentendorf

Chinon

Fessenheim

AUSTRIA

FRANCE

Lons-le-Saunier   Leibstadt   Lucens

Geneva

Creys-Malville   SWITZ   Goesgen

YUGOSLAVIA

Bugey   Milan

Bilbao   Marnac

Munguia   Cruas

San Sebastian   Valance d'Agen   Pierrelatte   Grenoble

Tricostin

Lodéve   Avignon

Vitoria   Verfeil

Pamplona   Marseilles   Toulon

Soria   Seyne-sur-Mer

ITALY

Capalbio

Madrid   Asco   Barcelona

Montalto di Castro

Molise

ALBANIA

GREECE

Valencia

**Protests against nuclear power
and mining and transport of
nuclear material: to early 1980**

strikes

occupations

sabotage

serious battles with
the police

demonstrations

one

two

three or more

Nuclear power states

present

planned (by 1984)

Source: Press reports
Keesings Contemporary Archives
Anna Gyorgy and friends,
No Nukes: Everyone's Guide to
Nuclear Power, 1979

Separatist, regionalist and irridentist movements late 1970s

separatist movements
active   dormant

regionalist movements
active   dormant

irridentist movements
active   dormant

active area

Source: G. Ashworth ed., Case Studies on Human Rights
and Fundamental Freedoms, Vols. I-V, 1975-76
World Minorities, Vols. I and II, 1977
Minority Rights Group
B. Crozier, Annual of Power and Conflict, 1975-76 •
Keesings Contemporary Archives
Press reports

61. Nationalism Against the Nation State

inset 1

The Case of the Kurds

TURKEY

SYRIA

IRAQ

IRAN

UNION OF SOVIET SOCIALIST REPUBLICS

see map 62

MONGOLIA

inset 1

TURKEY

CYPRUS
LEBANON
SYRIA

ISRAEL

IRAN

IRAQ

JORDAN

KUWAIT

EGYPT

inset 2

SAUDI
ARABIA

QATAR
U.A.E.

OMAN

AFGHANISTAN

Arabs

Pathans

PAKISTAN

Baluchis

Kashmir

Tibet

CHINA

NEPAL

INDIA

Mizoram

Chakmas
BANGLADESH

Nagaland

Kachins

Shans

Meo

Karens

BURMA

THAILAND

LAOS

KAM

VIETNAM

N
KOREA
S

JAPAN

TAIWAN

Taiwanese

HONG KONG

PHILIPPINES

N

KOREA

S

Tamilnad

Tamils
SRI LANKA

Muslim Malays

Sabah

Sarawak

MALAYSIA
SINGAPORE

INDONESIA

South
Molucca

Papuans

PAPUA
NEW GUINEA

East-Timor

SUDAN

inset 3

N
YEMEN

S
YEMEN

DJIBOUTI

South

ETHIOPIA

SOMALIA

KENYA

Somalis

UGANDA

RWANDA

Hutu

TANZANIA

COMOROS

MADAGASCAR

MALAWI

ZIMBABWE

MOZAMBIQUE

inset 2

TURKEY

Turks

Greek

Maronites

ISRAEL

Palestinians

JORDAN

SYRIA

IRAQ

SAUDI
ARABIA

inset 3

Eritrea

N
YEMEN

S
YEMEN

Somalis

Tigre

ETHIOPIA

Somalis

Harar &
Wollo

SOMALIA

AUSTRALIA

NEW
ZEALAND

East Siberian Sea

Laptev Sea

o Ukta

R Kolyma

R Indigirka

R Lena

YAKUT

Petropavlosk-Kamchatskiy

R Alden

o Yakutsk

Sea of Okhotsk

Lower Tunguska

b

Stony Tunguska

JEWS to Jewish Autonomous Oblast

R Amur

Birobidjan   o Khabarovsk

BURYAT

Blagoveshchensk

L Baykal

Irkutsk   o Ulan-Ude

Vladivostok

o Kyzyl

TUVA

ESTONIANS
KARELS
SAAMI
LATVIANS
LITHS
BYELO-
RUSSIANS
UKRAINIANS
R U S S I A N S
KOMI
MANSI
KHANTY
YAKUTS
BASHKIRS
K A Z A K H S
GEORGIANS
ARMENIANS
AZERS
BURYATS
BURYATS
KAZAKHS
KAZAKHS
TURKMEN
UZBEKS   KIRGIZ
TURKMEN   TADZHIKS

nonstrations

show trials

on nationalism

nd prison camps

oitals

● Balts	○ Paleo-Asiatics
○ Caucasians	● Slavs
● Finno-Ugrians	● Turkic
○ Iranians	○ sparsely populated
● Mongols	

Legend:

**Legal status of abortion
mid 1978**

on demand, but only for certain categories of women and/or for the initial stages of pregnancy

legal on social or social/medical grounds

legal on broad medical, juridical or eugenic grounds

legal on narrow medical or juridical grounds

illegal without exception

data not available

HONG KONG

SINGAPORE

Source: C. Tietze, Induced Abortion: 1979, New York, Population Council, 3rd ed.

inset

TURKEY
CYPRUS
SYRIA
LEBANON
IRAQ
ISRAEL
EGYPT
JORDAN
SAUDI ARABIA

UNION OF SOVIET SOCIALIST REPUBLICS

TURKEY
CYPRUS
SYRIA
LEBANON
ISRAEL
IRAQ
IRAN
EGYPT
inset
KUWAIT
QATAR
UAE
SAUDI ARABIA
OMAN
N YEMEN
S YEMEN
SUDAN
ETHIOPIA
SOMALIA
UGANDA
KENYA
TANZANIA
MALAWI
MADAGASCAR
MBABWE
MOZAMBIQUE

AFGHANISTAN
PAKISTAN
NEPAL
BHUTAN
INDIA
B-DESH
BURMA
SRI LANKA

MONGOLIA

CHINA

N KOREA
S KOREA
JAPAN

TAIWAN

LAOS
THAILAND
KAM
VIETNAM

MALAYSIA

PHILIPPINES

INDONESIA

PAPUA NEW GUINEA

AUSTRALIA

NEW ZEALAND

Changes in Abortion 1963-78

- liberal policy or law before 1963
- significant change to more liberal law or policy
- significant change to more restrictive law or policy
- no significant change, or data not available

- FIJI
- HONG KONG
- PAPUA NEW GUINEA
- SINGAPORE
- WESTERN SAMOA

**Major student disruptions
1968-69**

★ site of disruption

Source: Press reports
Keesing's Contemporary Archives, 1968-69
and various books

**Student enrolment at universities
and equivalent institutions
1968 or nearest year**

under 10,000

10,000 - 200,000

200,000 - 500,000

over 500,000

data not available

Source: UNESCO Statistical Yearbooks 1972, 1975

© Copyright Pluto Press

CANADA

UNITED STATES OF AMERICA

BERMUDA

inset

FRANCE

PORTUGAL

Madrid

SPAIN

Lisbon

ALGERIA

inset

PORTUGAL   SPAIN

ICELAND

NORWAY   SWED

DENMARK   *inset*

IRELAND   UNITED
KINGDOM   NETH   W   E
BELG   GERMANY   CZEC
AUS

FRANCE   SW   ITALY   YUGOS
ALB

TUNISIA

MOROCCO   ALGERIA   LIB

MAURITANIA   MALI   NIGER

GAMBIA   SENEGAL   GUINEA   UPPER
VOLTA   NIGERIA

SIERRA LEONE   IVORY
COAST   Accra   BENIN   Lagos

Monrovia   GHANA   TOGO   CAMEROON
LIBERIA   EQUATORIAL GUINEA

GABON   CONGO

ANG

NAMI

MEXICO

BAHAMAS

CUBA

JAMAICA   HAITI   DOMINICAN REPUBLIC
PUERTO RICO

GUATEMALA   HONDURAS   NICARAGUA
EL SALVADOR

Managua   BARBADOS
GRENADA

PANAMA   TRINIDAD AND TOBAGO
COSTA RICA   VENEZUELA

ECUADOR   COLOMBIA   GUYANA   SURINAM

PERU

BRAZIL

BOLIVIA

PARAGUAY

CHILE

URUGUAY

Santiago   Buenos Aires

ARGENTINA

MAURITIUS
Port Louis

★   site of urban upheaval

Widespread urban upheaval or strike
action involving major industrial
centres in the 1970s

once   twice   three   four or more
times   times

change in government or government policy
resulting from major urban upheaval

*Source: Keesings Contemporary Archives
Press reports*

© Copyright Pluto Press

The States of the World

Sovereign states and dependent territories referred to in this atlas
*Dependent territories

Afghanistan	Democratic Republic of Afghánistán
Albania	Republika Popullore Socialiste e Shqipërisë
Algeria	El Djemhouria El Djazaïria Eddemokratia Echaabia
Andorra	Les Vallées d'Andorra
	Valls d'Andorra
Angola	Angola
Antigua	Antigua
Argentina	República Argentina
Australia	Australia
Austria	Republik Österreich
Bahamas	The Commonwealth of the Bahamas*
Bahrain	Bahrain
Bangladesh	People's Republic of Bangladesh
Barbados	Barbados
Belgium	Royaume de Belgique
	Koninkrijk België
Belize	Belize*
Benin	République Populaire du Benin
Bermuda	Bermuda*
Bhutan	Druk-yul
Bolivia	República de Bolivia
Botswana	Botswana
Brazil	República Federativa do Brasil
Brunei	Brunei
Bulgaria	Narodna Republika Bulgaria
Burma	Pyidaungsu Socialist Thammada Myanma Naingngandaw
Burundi	Burundi
Cambodia *see* **Kampuchea**	
Cameroon	République Unie du Cameroun
Canada	Canada
Cape Verde	República de Cabo Verde
Cayman Islands	Cayman Islands*
Central African Republic	Central African Republic
Chad	République du Tchad
Chile	República de Chile
China	Zhonghua Renmin Gonghe Guo (People's Republic of China)
Colombia	República de Colombia
Comoros	Etat Comorien
Congo	République Populaire du Congo
Costa Rica	República de Costa Rica
Cuba	República de Cuba
Cyprus	Kypriaki Dimokratia
	Kibris Cumhuriyeti
Czechoslovakia	Československá Socialistická Republika
Denmark	Kongeriget Danmark
Djibouti	Republic of Djibouti
Dominica	Commonwealth of Dominica
Dominican Republic	República Dominicana
Ecuador	República del Ecuador
Egypt	Arab Republic of Egypt
El Salvador	República de El Salvador

Equatorial Guinea	República de Guinea Ecuatorial
Ethiopia	Ethiopia
Falkland Islands	Falklands Islands and Dependencies*
Fiji	Fiji
Finland	Suomen Tasavalta
	Republiken Finland
France	République Française
French Guiana	Guyane Française*
Gabon	République Gabonaise
Gambia	The Gambia
Guadeloupe	Guadeloupe*
Germany, East	Deutsche Demokratische Republik
	(German Democratic Republic)
Germany, West	Bundesrepublik Deutschland
	(Federal Republic of Germany)
Ghana	Ghana
Gilbert Islands *see* **Kiribati**	
Greece	Elliniki Dimokratia
Greenland	Grønland*
Grenada	Grenada
Guatemala	República de Guatemala
Guinea	République Populaire at Révolutionnaire de Guinée
Guinea-Bissau	Guinea-Bissau
Guyana	Guyana
Haiti	République d'Haiti
Honduras	República de Honduras
Hong Kong	Hong Kong*
Hungary	Magyar Népköztársaság
Iceland	Lýðveldið Ísland
India	Bharat
Indonesia	Republik Indonesia
Iran	Jumhouriy Islamiy Irân
	Islamic Republic of Iran
Iraq	al Jumhouriya al 'Iraqia
Ireland	Éire
Israel	Medinat Israel
	(State of Israel)
Italy	Repubblica Italiana
Ivory Coast	République de Côte d'Ivoire
Jamaica	Jamaica
Japan	Nippon (or Nihon)
Jordan	Al Mamlaka al Urduniya al Hashemiyah
	(The Hashemite Kingdom of Jordan)
Kampuchea	Democratic Kampuchea (formerly Cambodia)
Kenya	Djumhuri ya Kenya
Kiribati	Kiribati (formerly Gilbert Islands)
Korea, North	Chosun Minchu-chui Inmin Konghwa-guk
Korea, South	Han Kook
Kuwait	Dowlat al Kuwait
Laos	Laos
Lebanon	al-Jumhouriya al-Lubnaniya
Lesotho	Lesotho
Liberia	Liberia
Libya	Al-Jamahirayah Al-Arabiya
	Al Libya Al Shabiya Al-Ishtirakiya
	(Socialist People's Libyan Arab Jamahiriyah)

Liechenstein
Grand-Duché de Luxembourg

The Democratic Republic of Madagascar
Malawi
Malaysia
Republic of Maldives
République du Mali
Republika Ta Malta
Martinique*
République Islamique de Mauritanie
Mauritius
Estados Unidos Mexicanos
Monaco
Bügd Nayramdakh Mongol Ard Uls
(Mongolian People's Republic)
al-Mamlaka al-Maghrebia
The People's Republic of Mozambique

South-West Africa*
Suidwes-Afrika*
Nauru
Népal
Koninkrijk de Nederlanden

New Zealand
República de Nicaragua
République du Niger

Nigeria	Federal Republic of Nigeria
Norway	Kongeriket Norge
Oman	Saltanat Oman
Pakistan	Islamic Republic of Pakistan
Panama	República de Panamá
Papua New Guinea	Papua New Guinea
Paraguay	República del Paraguay
Peru	República del Perú
Philippines	República de Filipinas
	Republika ñg Pilipinas
Poland	Polska Rzeczpospolita Ludowa
Portugal	República Portuguesa
Puerto Rico	Puerto Rico*
Qatar	State of Qatar
Reunion	La Réunion*
Rhodesia see Zimbabwe	
Romania	Republica Socialistă România
Rwanda	Rwanda
St Christopher (St Kitts)-Nevis-Anguilla	St Christopher (St Kitts)-Nevis-Anguilla*
St Lucia	St Lucia*
St Vincent	St Vincent and the Grenadines*
San Marino	Repubblica di San Marino
Sao Tome and Principe	São Tomé e Principe
Saudi Arabia	al-Mamlaka al-'Arabiya as-Sa'udiya
Senegal	République du Sénégal
Seychelles	Seychelles
Sierra Leone	Sierra Leone
Singapore	Republic of Singapore
Solomon Islands	Solomon Islands
Somalia	Al-Jumhouriya As-Somaliya Al-Democradia
	(Somali Democratic Republic)

South Africa	Republiek van Suid-Afrika
	Republic of South Africa
South-West Africa *see* **Namibia**	
Spain	Estado Español
Sri Lanka	Sri Lanka
Sudan	Jamhuryat es-Sudan Al Democratia
	(The Democratic Republic of the Sudan)
Surinam	Suriname
Swaziland	Swaziland
Sweden	Konungariket Sverige
Switzerland	Suisse
	Svizzera
	Schweiz
Syria	al-Jamhouriya al Arabia as-Souriya
Taiwan	Republic of China
Tanzania	United Republic of Tanzania
Thailand	Prathes Thai
	Muang-Thai
Togo	République Togolaise
Tonga	Tonga (Friendly Islands)
Trinidad and Tobago	Trinidad and Tobago
Tunisia	Al-Djoumhouria Attunusia
Turkey	Türkiye Cumhuriyeti
Tuvalu	Tuvalu
Uganda	Uganda
Union of Soviet Socialist Republics (USSR)	Soyuz Sovyetskikh Sotsialisticheskikh Respublik
United Arab Emirates	United Arab Emirates
United Kingdom	United Kingdom of Great Britain and Northern Ireland
United States of America (USA)	United States of America
Upper Volta	République de Haute-Volta
Uruguay	República Oriental del Uruguay
Vanuatu Republic	Vanuatu Republic (formerly New Hebrides)
Vatican City	Vatican City State
Venezuela	República de Venezuela
Vietnam	Công Hòa Xã Hôi Chu Nghĩa Viêt Nam
	(The Socialist Republic of Vietnam)
Virgin Islands (British)	British Virgin Islands
Western Samoa	Samoa i Sisifo
Yemen, North	al Jamhuriya al Arabiya al Yamaniya
	(Yemen Arab Republic)
Yemen, South	Jumhurijah al-Yemen al Dimuqratiyah al Sha'abijah
	The People's Democratic Republic of Yemen
Yugoslavia	Socijalisticka Federativna Republika Jugoslavija
	(Socialist Federal Republic of Yugoslavia)
Zaire	République du Zaïre
Zambia	Zambia
Zimbabwe	Zimbabwe

Source: Statesman's Yearbook 1980–81, with amendments indicated by changed circumstances, e.g. Vanuatu, Iran; or by different interpretations of unchanged circumstances, e.g. Namibia

Notes to the Maps

This map shows the proliferation of states since 1945, when much of the world was still run from Europe. A further state, Vanuatu (the New Hebrides), became independent in July 1980, and the existence of powerful separatist movements (see *Map 61: Nationalism Against the Nation State*) suggests that the process of proliferation is still far from over.

A list of the many states with a population of less than a million is given on the map. For comparison, the estimated population of China in 1979 was 850 million, and that of India in 1979, 605 million.

Sovereign states are those that are generally accepted as such by other sovereign states and by international agencies. Thus Taiwan is included, although the governments of both China and Taiwan continue to insist that the island is an integral part of China. Similarly, both the Transkei and the Ukraine are excluded: the first is recognized only by South Africa, and the second, while recognized by the UN, is not deemed independent by any member state. In addition, there are border regions held by one sovereign state and claimed by another. The most notable example is Kashmir, which though incorporated into India is still claimed by Pakistan. No judgement is made on such disputes within this atlas and all states and boundaries conform to those given in *The Times Atlas of the World*.

The two Germanies are shown as new states because neither existed in its present form before 1945. It would have been even more misleading to have shown them as both existing, independently sovereign, in 1945.

Although Greenland is named to distinguish it from the neighbouring Canadian land mass, it is constitutionally part of Denmark. Likewise, Guadeloupe and Martinique, in the Caribbean, are constitutionally part of France.

Some longstanding European statelets, shown as insets on the left of the map, allow their foreign affairs to be controlled by powerful neighbours. They are not really states in the accepted sense at all.

2. The Proliferation of States

This map compares the populations of the world's states in 1979 and gives their annual average growth rate during the seventies.

Population is shown by a graphic distortion which preserves the geographical relationship between states. What emerges is an idea of how very different the world would look if the size of each state corresponded to its population. States with less than a million inhabitants have been excluded. A list of these is given on *Map 2: The Proliferation of States*.

Population growth rates are shown in colour. On current trends, a map of this kind produced year after year would show a marked and continuing decrease in the size of the rich states relative to the rest.

For other graphically distorted maps, which give a different view of the world, see for example *Map 23: National Income* or *Map 26: Government Income*.

For many states, population figures are no better than inspired guesses. In the US, for example, the existence of a large illegal immigrant society, officially estimated at between two and twelve million (see note to *Map 38: The Flight to Work*) is among the many factors in the widely recognized under-recording of population. In others, recording and non-recording of population forms part of the political tussle between its constituent parts — as between the states in Nigeria. In yet others there are simply no provisions for a separate census administration and population figures are supplied by officials engaged in other, seemingly more pressing, business and who have not necessarily been appointed for their numeracy.

3. The State by Population

4. The State Invades Antarctica

These four maps show the gathering invasion by the state system of the last large unpossessed land mass. They show Antarctica's potential mineral wealth, which states are claimants to its territory, and where each of those claimants has set up scientific stations. One US settlement, the Amundsen–Scott base at the South Pole, is at the meeting point of all the territorial claims in the continent, as if to underline the USA's refusal to recognize them.

Antarctica is rich in resources. It is already a major source of protein in the form of fish, whale meat and increasingly, krill (the many species of oceanic shrimp which constitute the basic food of whales). It holds promise of being a major source of the many minerals already mined in Southern Africa, Australia and South America with which Antarctica shares a common geological past. It is suspected of being rich in mineral oil and gas deposits. It also harbours 70 per cent of the world's fresh water which, in the form of ice, could be detached, towed and made available to the world's arid zones.

Antarctica is attractive in other ways. Scientifically, it is an isolated, relatively clean place from which to monitor global climatic conditions and changes, or levels of atmospheric pollution. It is also a useful base for research into human adaptability to extreme cold and dryness. Its remoteness is causing it to be viewed as a potential nuclear dustbin, able to absorb the radioactive waste that is too dangerous to store or to hide in the populated areas of the world. Militarily, it is attractive for its relative distance from likely theatres of war and its closeness to the only sea link between the Pacific, Atlantic and Indian Oceans other than the vulnerable Suez and Panama Canals.

5. The State Invades the Sea

'If a new and broadly accepted law of the sea does not emerge through international agreement, we face the prospect of each state determining its own view, with ever-widening claims to ocean space and resources. The acceptance of such a situation, favouring as it would power at the expense of justice, and risking unforeseeable possibilities of conflict, is unthinkable.' Kurt Waldheim, Secretary General, opening the sixth annual session of the Third United Nations Conference on the Law of the Sea, 15 May 1979.

This map shows how an extension of national jurisdiction to 200 nautical miles off all coasts, including those of islands, could affect as much as one-third of the sea area that covers some 70 per cent of the globe. Most littoral states have already claimed an Exclusive Economic Zone (EEZ) of 200 miles and, in some cases, the greater riches of the continental shelf have led to claims of 350 miles or more.

The many areas where EEZs overlap are areas of potential conflict. Some of these have caused disputes not yet resolved, and they are shown on the map. Where agreements have been reached (as between Britain and France for example) they have not been included.

The map also shows the areas of major fishing disputes between states, some of which date from pre-EEZ times. Such disputes, and similar disputes concerning sea-bed and undersea-bed resources, can only be fuelled by the new claims to hitherto free resources.

In the process of establishing and extending EEZs, small island territories have a special value. Some zones shown on the map have no apparent territorial source. This is because the islands which extend these EEZs are too small to show up on a map of this scale.

6. Invasions of the Sky

No state has so far claimed territorial rights to the stratosphere, and very few have invaded any part of it with people or materials. But the drive to do so is strong. By the end of the seventies, the pattern of satellite launches had become relatively fixed from year to year and this illustration gives an impressionistic view of launches made in 1978.

Two important and menacing developments took place in that year: the launching of the first hunter-killer satellite, and the contamination of a part of the earth's surface with radioactive debris from a satellite crash.

The satellite illustrated in the bottom right-hand corner of the map is one launched by the European Space Agency, which has eleven member states, whose shares range from Denmark's 2.19 per cent to West Germany's 25 per cent.

The relatively large number of Russian launches reflects the short life span of their satellites which, in contrast to US satellites, is usually measured in days rather than months.

It has been estimated that to the end of the seventies there have been roughly 2,000 launches, through which more than 11,300 man-made objects have been put into space: satellites, rockets, nose cones, shields, capsules and the like, along with fragments from the various space shots that went wrong.

Satellite tracking stations on earth have been overwhelmingly American. However, these are now becoming redundant as new techniques permit surveillance from fixed satellites, without the risk and dependence upon foreign governments and their citizens.

7. Foreign Military Presence

This map records all foreign air, land and sea bases at the end of the seventies. By its very nature, the subject is one on which those who have the information are most reluctant to part with it. It is also one in which abrupt changes in political alignment may lead to equally abrupt rearrangements of the bases which express and support them.

As a whole, the map shows that the global disposition of military forces not only reflects interstate alliances and old imperial interests, but also the fundamental confrontation between Western and Soviet bloc states.

Army bases are distinguished according to whether troops are stationed there primarily for fighting purposes or primarily for training, advisory or surveillance ones. Combat forces are divided into major and minor presences, namely, large self-contained forces organized as divisions of 10,000 or more (and occasionally, as in the case of Britain, 8,500 or more) and smaller forces of battalion strength or more.

It has been impossible to locate the precise sites of many foreign bases other than those of the Americans. Lack of information has also made it impossible to record the changes in tenancy of landing, refuelling and servicing facilities in the Middle East and the Horn of Africa, as Russians gave way to Americans in the last months of the seventies and the early months of 1980.

8. Military Spending

This map shows in colour, how much of each state's gross national product (GNP) is spent on military uses. Symbols are used to show the proportion of central government expenditure so employed. A regional summary is given in the inset map.

The source of these statistics is the US Arms Control and Development Agency, which tends to understate US arms expenditure (see the note to *Map 11: Arms for the Sake of the Profit*).

There is little correspondence between military spending and the nature of individual regimes. Many military regimes or regimes with a substantial military presence, as in Latin America for example, spend a relatively small proportion of their income on military purposes (see *Map 28: Military Government*). The financial cost of domestic repression over unarmed populations is small.

The real impulse to high military spending lies in global or regional confrontation between states. What the map shows overall is how much of the world's resources are devoted to unproductive preparations for war and to mutual destruction.

9. The Nuclear Club

This map shows the extent to which individual states are armed with deliverable nuclear weapons — on their own account or at the behest of an allied state.

A 'known nuclear weapons state' is one which has manufactured and exploded a nuclear weapon or other nuclear explosive device. A 'suspected nuclear weapons state' is one which is widely reputed to have constructed already, or to be able to construct within a very short time, several nuclear weapons. A 'near nuclear weapons state' is one which could develop this capability by the year 2000. An important component of this capability is the commissioning of a nuclear reactor, either for research or for the generation of electricity (see *Map 17: Nuclear Power*).

The danger in the proliferation of nuclear weapons has been underlined by Pakistan's public commitment to construct a nuclear weapon, despite considerable pressure from the main nuclear powers. This commitment is reportedly financed by Libya on the understanding that Libya would share in the result. And during the preparation of this atlas, Pakistan has leapt from being a rather distant candidate for the 'nuclear club' to being an imminent member.

10. Air Power

This map shows the comparative potency of individual states in conventional warfare. It uses the single but important index, numbers of combat aircraft. All naval and army combat aircraft are included, but not training, counter-insurgency and troop-carrying planes, or helicopters.

Numbers are by no means an invariable measure of potency. China's huge combat air force is seriously obsolescent; many of Egypt's aircraft, supplied by the Russians, are grounded for lack of spare parts; Iran's air force is increasingly understaffed and demoralized.

Yet the map provides the best comparison of potency in conventional warfare currently available. To have compared numbers of soldiers would have been to ignore the capacity of the weapons available to them, and this is often more material than the quantity of military personnel. Ownership of warships is limited to littoral states and is likely to be further influenced by the apparent vulnerability of coastal regions. As for land vehicles, it proved difficult to distinguish adequately between tanks and fighting vehicles; and among tanks, difficult to distinguish heavy, medium and light from one another.

11. Arms for the Sake of the Profit

This graphically distorted map shows the relative amounts spent by states on the purchase of foreign arms. Major arms exporters are distinguished from major external arms importers and, in the case of the latter, the major source of arms is shown in colour. The colour breakdown in the figures at the bottom of the map provides a regional summary of the size and source of arms imports.

The acquisition of weapons is an expensive business, and for those who are able to supply them, an extremely profitable one. Although even major arms suppliers, such as France and the United Kingdom, seem to dwindle beside the two giants in arms supply, the USA and the USSR, it does not follow that their trade is unimportant for them, or for their particular markets. Exports are, in fact, less crucial to the arms industry in the USA and USSR, which have huge domestic arms markets, than to states large parts of whose arms production is often ultimately dependent on the existence of export markets to supplement domestic ones.

Available statistics give different impressions of the USA's share of the arms market. The official US statistics which we have used, from the US Arms Control and Disarmament Agency, estimates the USA's share of world arms sales in 1976 at 39 per cent. While Tom Gervasi, in *Arsenal of Democracy* (New York, Grove Press 1977) attributes more than 50 per cent of such sales to the USA, and the *SIPRI Yearbook 1979*, 48 per cent.

The choice of major arms supplier is, for some states, not a static one. Since the statistics for this map were collected, for instance, both Egypt and Somalia have elected to buy the majority of their arms from the USA rather than the USSR.

This map is concerned solely with armed conflict between independent states in the seventies which involved uniformed personnel of the regular armed forces. It shows both the participants in such wars and the actual area of conflict. For internal armed conflict, see *Map 61: Nationalism Against the Nation State*.

Of course, the nature of such conflicts and their impact on the protagonists has differed enormously: from minor border clashes, as between Libya and Egypt, to the so-called Yom Kippur war in the Middle East, the wars between India and Pakistan and the long Vietnam war which was fought as well in both Kampuchea and Laos.

States are depicted as they were in early 1980; they may not have existed or existed in their current form at the time of some of the conflicts shown. Bangladesh was not an independent state during one of the wars between India and Pakistan. And it was the armed forces of Rhodesia that were engaged against Zambia and Mozambique before Zimbabwe was recognized as an independent state in 1980.

12. States at War in the 1970s

Thirteen minerals of generally accepted economic and strategic importance have been chosen to illustrate the disparity in the distribution of the world's mineral resources among states. Three of the most important minerals are dealt with elsewhere: in an inset map to *Map 15: Energy Power* (coal); *Map 16: Oil Power*; and *Map 59: Panic Stations* (gold). Of the minerals included in these two maps: antimony is used in the manufacture of batteries and, increasingly, as a flame retardant; and manganese is important not only as a steel hardening agent but also in the chemical industry.

Possession of a large quantity of a single important mineral does not necessarily convey a corresponding economic strength. In many instances, mines may be owned by foreign-based transnational corporations (see *Map 36: The Nationality of Transnationals*) which as far as possible dispose of resources in their own interests. Furthermore, market forces may so adjust the current value of particular minerals as to turn a major mine from a highly prized and profitable operation into a vulnerable, loss-making one. None the less, there are five states (shown in Map 14) whose abundance and diversity of mineral resources makes it appropriate to term them mineral powers: Australia, Canada, South Africa, the USA and the USSR.

In some states, the statistics for diamond production do not distinguish between gem and industrial stones. For this reason, the combined figure is given in all cases. South Africa dominates the international market in gem stones: partly through its own important share of world production; partly through its control of the Namibian mines; and not least because, through the Central Selling Organization, it commands an effective world monopoly to whose operations the USSR, amongst others, is party.

A reservation must be made with regard to the figures for chrome. During the period of UDI, from 1964 to 1980, some chrome mined in Zimbabwe, then Rhodesia, was almost certainly exported via South Africa and included in that country's statistics.

13. Mineral Power

14. The World Mineral Powers

This map shows the relationship between each state's energy consumption and production. States with a small or large energy surplus (those which produce more than they consume) are contrasted with states which have a small or large energy deficit (those which consume more than they produce).

The existence of an energy deficiency helps to explain certain policies. The enormous dependence of Japan on imported sources of energy has led to the Japanese government committing itself to a doubling of nuclear power generating capacity within the next few years. (See *Map 17: Nuclear Power.*)

Since the statistics for this map were prepared, the exploitation of rich oil deposits has been substantially changing the ratios of energy pro-

15. Energy Power

duction and consumption for some states: for instance, Mexico, Norway and the United Kingdom. However, this process has not affected the usefulness of the broad categories employed in the map.

Some comment on the statistics used is necessary:

Renewable energy sources, such as solar, tidal and wind power, which require advanced technology for their development, have been so neglected as to be considered negligible and are excluded by the source of the map, *UN World Energy Supplies 1973–77*. Traditional sources, such as wood and dung, are also excluded. Where their contribution is important, as in India and some African states, no accurate figures are available. Where such figures are available, as for some European states, their relative contribution is unimportant.

Production data are based on the production of coal, lignite, crude petroleum, natural gas, natural gas liquids, hydro- and nuclear electricity. Where peat is important as fuel, it is included.

Consumption data are based on the apparent consumption of coal, lignite, petroleum products, natural gas, hydro- and nuclear electricity. Coke, manufactured gas, and electricity traded internationally are considered to have been consumed by importing countries.

Comparison between coal and other sources of energy is based on calorific value. One metric ton of coal is equivalent to 1.47 metric tons of crude petroleum or 1.67 metric tons of natural gas liquid.

The steeply rising price of oil has caused renewed interest in the world's coal resources. Coal can be used as a substitute fuel for power stations and is itself a source of oil. The inset map compares coal production and consumption in all states where it is above 10 million metric tons a year.

16. Oil Power

This map compares the oil production and consumption of individual states where it amounts to more than 0.5 per cent of the world's total. Annual average rates of growth or decline are shown in colour and major oil movements, in proportion to their size, are shown in all cases where they are above 5 million metric tons.

The soaring price of oil during the seventies has given the major oil-exporting states enormous economic power. The Organization of Petroleum Exporting Countries (OPEC) first used its united weight in 1973. Since then, even those oil exporters which have remained outside the cartel, such as Mexico and the United Kingdom, have effectively accepted its leadership in setting prices. Saudi Arabia is by far the largest oil exporter in the world and among OPEC members it is by far the most influential. The United States has publicly and repeatedly pressed Saudi Arabia to use this influence to hold down oil prices. But fear of damaging the cartel and other regional political constraints have qualified Saudi Arabia's ability to do so.

The increasing dependence of the United States on imported oil has been a crucial factor in its persistently enormous trade deficit in the post war period. This has led to the depreciation of the US dollar against many currencies, the erosion of confidence in the dollar as a reserve currency, and an international monetary upheaval without precedent since the second world war. This upheaval is the subject of *Map 59: Panic Stations.*

At present the USSR is still a major oil exporter. But reliable estimates suggest that within a few years it will, like the USA, be an oil importer on an increasing scale. The economic and political consequences of a scramble by the two superpowers for scarce and costly oil supplies are unlikely to be comfortable.

17. Nuclear Power

Two major factors contribute to the current rush by states to develop nuclear power stations. First, growing energy deficits exacerbated by the rising price of oil, and second, the access that such programmes offer to the production of nuclear weapons (see *Map 10: The Nuclear Club*). There is no doubt that the latter is a significant inducement for some poor states, with a relatively low energy consumption, to undertake ambitious nuclear power programmes.

By 1978, 5.85 per cent of the world's total electricity generating power already came from nuclear power stations. This proportion will increase dramatically if all the power stations planned are put into operation.

Only nuclear power reactors likely to produce more than 20 megawatts (mW(e)) per year are included and the information on planned nuclear reactors is, of course, liable to rapid change.

For public response to the dangers of such programmes, see *Map 60: Nuclear Power No Thanks.*

18. Food Power

In this graphically distorted map, colour is used to show whether states have a small or large deficit in food trade. The size of each state is related to its share of world food trade in 1977; if a state is a net exporter, its size is determined by its share of world food exports; if a net importer, by its share of world food imports.

The main exporters of staple grains — the USA, Canada, Australia and Argentina — can use their food surplus as an instrument of considerable power. The US Secretary of State for Agriculture, Earl Butz, said in 1974, 'Food is a weapon. It is now one of the principal weapons in our negotiating kit.' In 1980, in response to the Russian invasion of Afghanistan, the USA embargoed all sales of grain to the USSR not already pledged by contract.

Some states may well show an overall surplus in food trade and yet be unable to nourish their populations at all adequately. Such surpluses are in many cases created by large exports of a single food or beverage commodity, especially coffee, cocoa, sugar and honey, or tropical fruits (see *Map 21: Dependence and Diversity*). Comparison should also be made with *Map 44: Our Daily Bread.* Colombia, a major coffee exporter, is shown here to have a substantial surplus in food trade. Yet the number of calories available per head of population is below requirement and there was a famine in Colombia in 1967. Africa's case is even more ironic. Here it is shown to have an overall surplus in food trade as a result of major exports of coffee, cocoa and tropical fruits. Yet it remains one of the world's most desperate areas of undernourishment and even starvation.

19. Industrial Power

This map shows the enormous discrepancies in industrial wealth, and the power associated with it, between a relatively small number, and the vast mass of the world's states. Canada, for example, with a population of 23 million has more industrial power than the whole of Africa and India combined. The map shows too, the enormous industrial dominance of the USA, although it is diminishing in relation to Japan and the main industrial states of Western Europe. (See also *Map 55: Industrial Droop* which shows the generally decreasing rates of industrial growth between the sixties and the seventies.)

In this map, as elsewhere in this atlas, the need for manageable bands of comparison produces a low band which contains considerable disparities. As an extreme example, the Central African Republic, with an industrial output of US$46 million per year in the mid-seventies is bracketed with Egypt, whose annual industrial output was US$4,000 million.

The statistics available for industrial output are surprisingly inadequate in a number of ways. The only comprehensive figures are given in the UN *Yearbook of Industrial Statistics*, but these apply to different years, many states are omitted altogether, and different criteria are employed. They also demonstrate the distortions inevitable when local values are translated into some international standard, in this case the US dollar. Several East European states have two separate and official dollar conversion rates for their currencies: a 'basic' one, and a non-commercial rate, generally for tourists. The UN statistics have been calculated according to the basic rate, but if these were comparable, the value of manufacturing output in Poland, for example, would have been close to that of West Germany. For the purposes of this map such figures have been converted according to the non-commercial rate.

20. Technological Power

The number of scientists and engineers which each state has in relation to its total population is clearly linked to the size of its manufacturing output – as comparison with *Map 19: Industrial Power* shows. Industrial powers have much greater resources with which to sustain and promote research and development. The inset map, *Brain Drain*, adds the point that there is an international flow of skilled professional and technical labour from the poor states to the rich – labour which is trained at the expense of the poor to benefit the rich.

Given the lacklustre performance in manufacturing output of some East European states, such as Poland and Czechoslovakia, it may seem strange that they should possess so high a proportion of scientists and engineers: as high as Japan and twice as high as West Germany. The answer must lie in their wasteful use of all resources, human as well as material, under the dominion of a distended bureaucracy.

One important aspect of technological power not portrayed on the map is ownership of patents and trademarks. The rich states extend their dominion in technology by either preventing access to certain processes or by exacting a high price for them. Of the patents granted to foreigners in 50 poor states in 1972, no less than 40.6 per cent were owned in the USA, 11.5 per cent in West Germany, 9.6 per cent in Switzerland and 8.9 per cent in the United Kingdom. Of the trademarks registered by foreigners in 54 poor states in 1974, no less than 34.3 per cent were owned in the USA, 15.1 per cent in Japan, 12.2 per cent in the United Kingdom, 9.2 per cent in West Germany and 7 per cent in France. (UNCTAD, *The Role of the Patent System*, 1975 and *The Impact of Trademarks on the Development Process of Developing Countries*, 1977).

21. Dependence and Diversity

This map shows how many states are dependent, for the majority of their export income, on the sale of either one product or a very small number of products. The most extreme case is Oman, where the whole of its export income comes from oil.

The economic weakness of a state dependent upon a single major export is self-evident, especially when it is poor, in competition with other poor states and with the rich as well, and when the product is an agricultural commodity. Not only is there the persistent threat of bad or too bountiful harvests, there is also the threat that access to major traditional markets might be denied: when major customers are also a producer, as with sugar for example, they can take steps to protect their own production at others' expense.

Some poor countries appear to have a stronger, more diversified economic base than they have in reality, since their principal export also takes a partly manufactured form. Bangladesh offers a striking example: 25 per cent of its export income comes from raw jute; but another 25 per cent comes from textile products made mainly from jute and a further 33 per cent comes from woven non-cotton textiles, which are also mainly made of jute. A rare example among rich states is New Zealand: fully two-thirds of New Zealand's exports are animal products.

It should be noted that the statistics do not include tourism nor do they include income from the services offered by tax havens (see *Map 37: The Islands of the Blessed*). For some states, notably in the Caribbean, these are a substantial source of foreign income.

22. Trade Power

This is a graphically distorted map which reveals the extent to which international trade is dominated by a relatively few rich states. In 1978, the whole of Africa emerges as less powerful in trading terms than the

United Kingdom; and the whole of South and Central America as less powerful than the Netherlands.

By comparing this map with *Map 19: Industrial Power* and *Map 23: National Income*, it can be seen that the United States is comparatively weaker in international trade than it is either in manufacturing output, or in the value of its gross national product.

The USSR's relative weakness as a trading power — compared, say, with population (see *Map 3: The State by Population*) with industrial output (see *Map 19: Industrial Power*) or with military power (see *Map 8: Military Spending*) — is also apparent.

As *Map 21: Dependence and Diversity* shows, the weakness of the small trading states is compounded by their dependence on one or two export commodities. Because the poor countries are marginal to international trade, they remain poor; because they are poor, they remain marginal.

23. National Income

The gross national product (GNP) of states in 1977 is shown by a graphic distortion which preserves, as in other maps of this kind, the geographical relationship between states. The annual average rate of growth or decline in GNP per head is shown in colour. (GNP measures a country's total annual income including net earnings from abroad.) What the map underlines is the vast discrepancies between states in both national income and rate of growth.

The most notable increases in the growth rate of GNPs during the seventies have generally been due to one of two factors: either the possession of oil (see *Map 16: Oil Power*); or, participation in the international assembly line of manufacture, where much of the processing has increasingly gone to states able to provide a skilled, controlled, and relatively low-paid labour force, along with tax concessions (see *Map 37: Islands of the Blessed*).

The inset map, *People and Purses*, shows the amount of GNP, or national income, available per head of population. Of course, the greater a state's population, the more it must earn to sustain the well-being of its people.

National income statistics must be viewed with particular caution as pointed out in the Introduction. They do not measure adequately either the value of subsistence production or the value of domestic labour. Further, the measure of national income statistics is the national currency of a single state, the USA, which is vulnerable to movements in foreign exchange rates. To say that the national income of Switzerland, for instance, has increased within a few days by 1 per cent because the Swiss franc has risen in that proportion against the US dollar is manifestly absurd. Yet it is standard practice in national income comparisons.

24. The Debt-Laden South

It is by now well-known that most poor states, generally situated in the southern part of the world, are becoming poorer in relation to the rich, generally situated in the northern part of the world. This map measures the extent of the accumulated debt of poor states, and the degree to which that debt has recently grown or declined. The inset map shows the drain on export income of debt servicing charges and debt repayments.

What the map as a whole shows is the increasing instability of an international economic system in which many states are unable to live within their straitened means, let alone develop their economies — and in which the related fear of debt repudiation and state bankruptcy fuels the further growth of debt. (For manifestations of this increasing instability see *Map 58: Credit Runs Riot* and *Map 59: Panic Stations*.)

In many instances, obligations to foreign creditors can be met only by contracting new debts, thereby increasing the overall burden with its corresponding drain on future income. When creditors are unwilling to provide more loans, as has happened already to both Zaire and Turkey, formal bankruptcy can only be avoided by postponing debt repayments.

An increase in debt does not invariably mean an increase in economic vulnerability. Mexico and Venezuela, for example, have found no difficulty in borrowing huge sums of money in the expectation (shared by their creditors) of future income from oil exports. At the same time, however, the oil price rises that enhance the economic prospects of a Mexico or a Venezuela add correspondingly to the difficulties and costs of other states.

To be sure, among the states affected by the weight of debt are many in the rich northern part of the world. And likewise, such states are driven to increase their external public debt. But the problems of rich industrial states are of a different order from those of the poor states. They are better able to regain a surplus in their balance of payments by increasing exports, especially to the oil exporting states.

25. Margins of Safety

This map shows the size of the gold and foreign currency reserves held by each state in relation to its monthly imports bill: how long each state could sustain its current level of imports without additional earnings from exports.

It must be emphasized that the same figure has a different significance for the rich and for the poor. States whose sources of export income are diverse have much greater flexibility than those dependent on income from one or very few products (see *Map 21: Dependence and Diversity*).

Gold and foreign exchange reserves represent a form of liquid capital to meet deficits in current payments and to repay debt. The gold content of reserves in the map was valued, according to the practice of the World Bank, at the 'official' price of US$ 42.2 per ounce. This is well below the average market price in the recent past. Some governments have accordingly revalued their gold holdings, but while this would make very little difference to the value of reserves held by the poor, it would greatly increase the value of reserves held by the rich — especially the USA, West Germany, France, the Netherlands, Italy and, of course, South Africa.

For reasons best known to themselves, the USSR and states in Eastern Europe do not disclose the value or content of their reserves.

26. Government Income

This graphically distorted map shows each state's share of total world-wide government income from taxes, levies and direct production. The annual average rate of growth or decline of this share is shown in colour.

Gross domestic product (GDP) measures the total wealth generated within a state each year. By comparison with gross national product (GNP), the subject of *Map 23: National Income*, it excludes income payable abroad and excludes income from foreign sources. Reservations on GNP statistics, given in the note to Map 23, apply equally to GDP figures, but additional reservations are needed here. Although the data for most states has been averaged out over a period of three years, 1975–77, for some states three-year comparisons were not available, and for others statistics had to be taken for earlier years. Further, in some cases the figure for a government's share of GDP dates from a different year to that of the GDP figure itself. It is very unlikely though that this invalidates the comparison.

Figures for the USSR and similar states are based differently from those for the rest of the world. We have used those that are closest to UN national income accounting practice.

The wealth of governments, of course, does not necessarily correspond to the wealth, let alone the size, of their respective populations. For comparison, see *Map 3: The State by Population* and *Map 23: National Income*.

27. The State Apparatus

This map shows the number of people, as a proportion of total population, employed by each state for the purpose of internal security.

Some states appear to include in their definition all those who perform police functions of any kind and this must explain the extra-ordinarily high figure for Sweden, for example – 3,655 members of internal security forces for each 100,000 population.

States which include various forms of people's militia or home guard in their statistics are identified on the map. Such forces are used to supplement conventional police. East Germany, for instance, has less than one hundred conventional police for every 100,000 inhabitants, but when the people's militia is included the figure soars to 2,443. Another interesting example is the United States, where a National Guard is used in such circumstances as serious rioting. In the USA, the number of conventional police is 299 per 100,000 population, but when the National Guard are included the figure rises to 515. Both Denmark and Portugal have sizeable 'home guards'. Finally, Switzerland's internal security forces include a large force of reservists which leads to the enormous figure of 7,766 for every 100,000 people. To show how such inclusions may distort the statistics one need only compare with these examples the figure for the United Kingdom of 44.7.

We would have preferred to portray the state apparatus in terms of administrative employment by central and local government, but astonishingly, relevant figures of any kind are available for very few states and when they are, they involve widely different definitions of government employees. In some cases workers in nationalized industries are included, along with teachers and soldiers; in others teachers and soldiers are included, but not workers in nationalized industries; in still others, only those directly involved in government administration are included, even excluding those administering state welfare schemes. As examples of the wide discrepancies in the statistics, official Russian figures for 1978 suggest that some two and a half million out of a total labour force of 109 million (or 2.16 per cent) belong to the apparatus of government, economic and cooperative management and public organizations. While official Danish figures suggest there are some 678,000 public employees out of an economically active population of two and a half million – over 26 per cent.

Such material as is available, and could be made consistent, is shown in the inset map. It includes employees in state health and welfare schemes, but excludes teachers, soldiers and workers in state or para-statal industries.

28. Military Government

This map shows the involvement of the military in the government of states, wherever it is substantial, at the end of 1978. The military have not stood still since then, of course. Idi Amin's regime in Uganda was overthrown only for its civilian successor to be displaced by a military coup. Liberia and Surinam both acquired military regimes in 1980 and South Korea, while retaining a civilian government facade, entered the eighties under military command.

A state under martial law is one in which the law governing the armed forces applies to the entire population. A military regime is one in which members of the armed forces compose the principal agency of government. A regime with 'substantial military participation' is one in which the principal agency of government may have a majority of civilians, but crucial positions, including some not directly connected with the armed forces, are held by members of the military. States with 'regimes (as at the end of 1978) established by military coup' have governments which have been essentially continuous since the coup which determined the regime.

Some states, for example Malawi, have civilian or largely civilian dictatorships which are to a greater or lesser degree dependent on military backing. These have not been included since they are not primarily instances of military government.

29. Bullets and Blackboards

This map shows the relative importance attached by states to invest-ment in soldiers and investment in teachers. It also shows the number of soldiers employed by each state in relation to its population.

The ratio of soldiers to population gives no indication of the size of individual armies. For such an impression, comparison should be made with *Map 3: The State by Population*. China, for example, may have a low ratio of soldiers to population, but so large is its population that it has more soldiers than any other state. Nor does a low ratio of soldiers to population necessarily denote a relatively libertarian regime or a relatively contented populace. The sustenance of oppression or the control of discontent often call on the employment not of soldiers but of special methods (see *Map 31: Scourges of the State*) and special agents (see *Map 27: The State Apparatus*).

Particular events may radically alter or at least temporarily distort information on individual states. For example, the overthrow of the fascist regime in Portugal ended a system of military conscription, for warfare abroad, which had made Portugal's ratio of soldiers to population among the highest in the world. And since 1974, the changing situation in South-East Asia produced first a large reduction and then a large increase in the relative sizes of the armies in the area.

30. Conscription and Conscience

This map shows the extent of compulsory military service for men in the mid seventies and the status of conscientious objection in the early seventies. In some states, military service is compulsory but selective and the colour for these has been cross-hatched with the colour for the appropriate period of service. Reserve duty is also shown.

In some states, for example Poland and the Netherlands, the length of compulsory service in the army differs from that in other branches of the armed forces. In such cases, it is the length of army service which has been taken as the standard. In other states, notably Sweden and Portugal, a flexible period of military service applies and here the shorter has been used.

In Israel and Burma conscription applies to women as well as men. There are signs that other states may adopt this practice. In some cases conscription applies to only a section of the population: in South Africa, only to whites; in Cyprus, only to Greeks; in Israel only to Jews and Druzes.

No state accepts political opinion as sufficient grounds for release from military service: conscientious objection is essentially regarded by states as a concession to be restricted as far as possible rather than as a right to be enjoyed. In many, even religious grounds are so circumscribed that only members of a particular sect qualify — for example, the Mennonites in Mexico, Bolivia and Paraguay.

31. Scourges of the State

A healthy society, Plato believed, would have no use for doctors or lawyers. By analogy, it may be argued that a world without states would have no need for the prisons, the torture chambers and the places of execution that this map records.

States rarely acknowledge the application of torture or the existence of political prisoners and in the reporting of these the work of Amnesty International is crucial. For this reason, though, it is important to emphasize that the absence of individual symbols on this map may only mean that there have been no reported instances in the years covered.

The law on the death penalty is sometimes misleading for a number of reasons. In the United Kingdom, for example, the death penalty remains on the statute book but for use only in cases of treason and certain forms of piracy. It has not been imposed since 1964 and is popularly believed to have been abolished altogether. The fact that it remains on the statute book, however, means that it may be much more readily reinstated. In other states, for example Australia and the USA, the death penalty comes within the jurisdiction of constituent states rather than the federal government. In both cases, some state governments have abolished the death penalty while others have retained it.

The number of prisoners in relation to total population is shown in colour. Some of the statistics are confusingly low and may well denote the very opposite of the contented, peaceful conditions they appear to indicate. In Amin's Uganda and Pol Pot's Kampuchea, for example, there were less protracted ways of dealing with opponents than confining them in jails.

32. Refugees

The world refugee population is large, fluctuating and poorly recorded. This map shows the numbers of new refugees between 1972 and 1979. Such refugees may either have been displaced within their own state or have been obliged to move to others across state frontiers.

Major refugee movements both before and since this period have not been included. For example, the Nigerian civil war over Biafra in 1967–1970 led to a major internal displacement of population; substantial flows of refugees have moved from Cuba to the USA both before and after the period; and since 1979 there have been regular reports of large numbers leaving Afghanistan and various provincial states in north-east India. A single exception has been made. The Palestinians have been included because of their continuing political importance and because, unlike so many other refugees, they have scarcely been resettled or absorbed.

33. Languages of Rule

A language of rule is one which is used by a political and/or economic elite to reinforce its control and sustain its cohesion. It effectively helps to deny participation in government or administration by those who do not speak it. It promotes, most notably in Africa, a closer association between the elites of individual states than with their own populations.

The map identifies the varying status of languages imported or created by such elites. It shows where such languages are official, where they are not official but widely used in government and business, and where they merely have status as old imperial languages. It also shows where popular, creole forms of old imperial languages have developed, particularly in the Caribbean, and where the majority of the poor are unable to speak the official language, as is the case with poor, indigenous Indian populations in parts of South America.

Where languages of rule have been imported their status as official languages may be temporary, as proved the case in Morocco (French) or as may happen throughout Malaysia (English), where in 1980, only Sarawak maintains English as an official language. In some countries – Ireland, the Lebanon and Tanzania – there are two or more official languages, only one of which is the language of the majority. This is shown by cross-hatching colours and adding symbols for the minority language or languages.

Greenland does not appear on this map but as a province of Denmark, Danish is its official language, while the majority of its population of 48,000 speak an Eskimo language.

The map is a contemporary rather than historical record. Portuguese, for example, was brought by conquest to what is now called Brazil. It then so far displaced the indigenous languages as to no longer constitute a language of rule.

34. Religions of Rule

The belief in future fulfilment, prosperity and security; the representation of that belief in ritual; its supporting justification by reference to holy writ, interpreted by a special category of people; and its accommodation within state-supported or state-associated institutions: such are the hallmarks of many religions. In this sense, official Marxism-Leninism is such a religion: with its concentration on the benefits of the future from the sacrifices of the present; its conventional parades and ceremonies; its revealed truths, whose texts are to be interpreted only by those appointed to do so; and its association with the power of the state. Furthermore, like some other religions, it has its own schismatic orthodoxies (the Moscow and the Peking denominations); its populist low church heterodoxies (Titoism in Yugoslavia); its anathematized heresy (Trotskyism); and its fundamentalist sects (revolutionary Marxism).

A religion of rule is defined as one which is professed by the governing classes and which sustains their solidarity. Poland provides a good example of the first case, since official Marxism-Leninism, of the Moscow denomination, rules over a population almost entirely Roman Catholic in allegiance. An example of the second case is the United Kingdom. Here the majority of the population is either secular or holds a variety of religious beliefs. But the Church of England is the official state religion, its bishops are automatically members of the upper house of parliament and it retains control through its official status.

In dealing with Christianity, Catholicism and Protestantism are distinguished only where one of these is clearly dominant, and no distinction is made between different versions of Protestantism. As far as Islam is concerned, the only distinction made is between Sunni and Shia, such variants as do exist being accommodated within each dominant strain.

Sites of recent religious conflict are shown on the map, but only where there is current violence on religious grounds, or where there is a significant religious component. In Kampuchea, this reflects the struggle between Peking- and Moscow-backed forces; in Afghanistan, between Islam and Moscow.

35. The Public and the Private

These two maps *Big Money* and *Big Business*, are intended to show the wealth, and therefore power, of some of the world's major banks and some of the largest transnationals compared with many independent states.

Big Money shows the gold and foreign currency reserves of individual states in relation to the assets of banks in the private sector (that is, not central banks). While it is normal for a bank's assets to be almost entirely equalled by its liabilities, it is almost always true that a state's national reserves are more than matched by its foreign debts.

Since the map was prepared, the Crédit Agricole de France replaced the Bank of America as the world's largest bank, with assets of US$105,000 million. Yet in 1976, no state had assets larger than the Bank of America and only one, West Germany, had assets above those of the National Westminster Bank, then only the twentieth in size. At the same time, although the Cantonal Bank of St Gall, in Switzerland, was the world's 300th bank in size, many states, especially in South America and Africa, had reserves lower than its assets.

The reserve figures for the United Kingdom are now considerably higher for a number of reasons: partly because the British government has pursued a tighter monetary policy with related high interest rates, and partly because North Sea oil and oil price rises have produced a strong currency and an enormous inflow of funds.

As with *Map 25: Margins of Safety*, it has been impossible to compare the national reserves of the USSR and associated states because they are not declared.

Big Business compares the gross national product of individual states with the sales income of a range of US transnationals, or multinationals, in 1977. While a corporation's turnover is not the precise equivalent of a state's GNP, the two are close enough for useful comparison. Both Guyana and Surinam, together with many states in Africa, had GNPs lower than the sales income of the US owned company, Time Inc.

36. The Nationality of Transnationals

This map demonstrates the dichotomy in the nature of transnational enterprise. While their name and their method of functioning would suggest allegiance to no particular state interests, they remain tied to the state where they are officially based. The pressures of world-wide competition lead transnational companies to cross state boundaries. The drive for power and the need for support from the state means that their 'nationality' should never be overlooked.

The map confirms common knowledge, that the majority of transnationals are owned in the states of Western Europe and, in particular, the United States, home base of the largest transnationals in the world.

This map shows some of the many ways in which corporations and business generally seek to avoid state taxation. It also shows how many states, especially islands in the Atlantic and the Pacific, find legal means of benefiting from this search. To emphasize the role of islands, all the states involved have been artificially depicted as such.

The map isolates tax havens, flags of convenience, free production zones and offshore manufacturing zones as the primary means of tax avoidance. It is in the nature of the topic that such a map cannot be exhaustive; private capital's search for havens of one sort or another is relentless, inventive, and often successfully cloaked in secrecy.

The difference between major and minor tax havens is one of financial importance, as judged by the private banking sources consulted.

States offering registration of flags of convenience are those which provide shipping companies with the advantages of nominal or low taxation, and little or no regulation of safety or working conditions on board.

Free production zones are areas set aside for offshore manufacturing or assembly plants. Major zones are defined as those in which 10,000 or more workers were employed in 1975. Offshore plants may operate both inside and outside free production zones. They are based on local labour but export all their output. They enjoy tax and customs privileges. The free production zones featured on this map relate to Africa, Asia and Latin America only. Others, in Ireland and, increasingly Eastern Europe, have been excluded on the grounds that they are as yet unimportant in their economic and social effect on their host economies.

This map shows the numbers of people prepared to go abroad in search of work, their states of origin and the states to which they are drawn.

While international agencies such as the United Nations and the International Labour Office in Geneva are permanently working to compile and publish statistics on population movements and employment, there is no single world-wide study of people seeking work across national frontiers. As a result this map has been produced in the full knowledge that it is incomplete, dependent as it is on occasional regional statistics and personal estimates of individuals. Some states, such as Australia, Venezuela and north-east India, are known to attract immigrant workers, but no figures or estimates were available.

One of the difficulties is that in some cases most of the people who enter a state in search of work do so illegally. This is particularly true of the United States where most illegal entrants do so from Mexico and most of these, perhaps two-thirds of the total, are Mexican citizens. Estimates of the illegal migrant population 'range from two to twelve million' according to a *White House Fact Sheet*, 4 August 1977. The figure on this map of three million migrant workers in the US is an estimate prepared by Roger Böhning of the ILO.

Migrant labour is a major source of income to both the families left behind and their states of origin. At the end of 1973, West Germany was paying children's allowances for some 850,000 children who were living abroad and who had at least one parent working in West Germany. These were going to the following:

Turkey	515,200
Yugoslavia	148,100
Italy	80,900
Spain	42,500
Portugal	32,600
Greece	28,700

37. The Islands of the Blessed

38. The Flight to Work

The number of foreign children who were resident in West Germany and receiving payments at the same time came to 154,400. (UN, *The Welfare of Migrant Workers and Their Families*, Report of a seminar in Yugoslavia, New York 1976.)

A further example of the value of migrant labour to their states of origin relates to African migrant workers in France. In 1973, transfers from migrant workers in France contributed 24.7 per cent of Morocco's total revenue from external sources, 20 per cent of Algeria's and 11.6 per cent of Tunisia's. (Roberto Aliboni ed., *Arab Industrialization and Economic Integration*, London, Croom Helm 1979.)

39. Exploitation

Ideally, a measure of exploitation would compare the output of all productive workers (i.e. workers whose labour results in essential ingredients for further production) with their income. Such a measure does not exist, since productive and unproductive workers are not differentiated analytically or statistically; since inessential is not differentiated from essential output; since statistics do not cover all economic activity, but only part of it; and since they are not truly international in their scope.

So instead of using a formula such as: value added in productive activity divided by wages in cash and kind for productive activity, we have had to settle for the following: value of gross output in manufacturing, less wages and salaries in manufacturing, divided by wages and salaries in manufacturing.

The results of applying the latter formula were divided into five levels of exploitation: first level – below 4; second level – 4 to 6.99; third level – 7 to 9.99; fourth level – 10 to 12.99; and fifth level – over 12.

The data itself presented certain problems. Some governments report the value of gross output at factor cost, the cost to the producer of the elements of production excluding indirect taxes but including subsidies; some, at producers' prices, including indirect taxes, but excluding subsidies; and some adopt hybrid definitions. Some governments make an attempt to quantify non-wage payments, most do not. In some states – the richer ones – salaries form a large component of the labour bill, in most they do not. In some states, manufacturing covers a far wider range of economic activity than in others. In most but not all cases, a three-year average was used, in others, the three most recent years available, and occasionally, less than three years.

Overall, it must be admitted, we believe that the available data gives a biased picture. Exploitation in rich states appears to be lower than exploitation in poor states, when the opposite may well be the case. It is to be hoped that this first world map of exploitation may lead to a more refined study.

40. The Labour Force

These two maps describe the nature of the labour force in individual states: *Workers on the Land* and *Workers in Industry*. Neither includes the service sector which, everywhere, although for very different reasons, is both large and growing.

Both maps confirm the dependence of poor states on agricultural labour and production. But some poor states, for example Zambia and Uganda, show a surprisingly small percentage of their population to be working in agriculture, together with an equally, and not surprising, small percentage working in industry. This is because in many poor states, much of what is termed 'economically active population' is actually unemployed or is engaged on the fringes of the economy in a multitude of subsistence 'service' capacities. Although this would appear to be a subject on which there would be fairly reliable and complete statistics, this is far from the case. Many African states clearly have great difficulty in establishing the nature of their workforces and may even be reluctant to reveal information.

Figures for China, which are not otherwise available, have been taken from estimates provided by Jon Sigurdson, in *Rural Industrialization in China*, Harvard 1977.

This map shows the percentage of women workers in the non-domestic labour force and gives an index of the degree of sexual discrimination in jobs.

In many states whose workforce is employed primarily in agriculture (see *Map 40: The Labour Force*), women workers inhabit a twilight zone between agricultural and domestic labour. This often leads to strange statistical conclusions such as the apparently low percentage of women workers in both Equatorial Guinea and Guinea-Bissau, and where the actual numbers are known to be high. By comparison, it would be expected that the number of women workers in Islamic states would be low and this is borne out by the map.

The index of sexual discrimination in jobs is based on the proportion of women (or men) who would have to change their occupational or industrial classification for there to be sex equality in employment. Inevitably, the definition of inequality involves an important component of status and this must reflect in some way the personal judgement of its source, Elise Boulding *et al.*, *Handbook of International Data on Women*, 1976. Yet the ranking confirms general knowledge: that women enjoy greater job equality in Eastern Europe than in Western Europe and that there is most discrimination in the Islamic states of the Middle East.

There is one major reservation to be made. Absence of discrimination in dangerous or debilitatingly heavy manual labour is not necessarily a sign of equality. In many Asian states, women act as unskilled assistants to more skilled male workers.

41. Women Workers

In this map we have attempted to peer behind the single concept of trade unionism to the widely differing realities of trade union freedom and confinement. In some states, trade unions are more or less independent bodies, able to take most decisions related to their interests without interference from the state, except in times of national emergency. In most states, whatever the official pretensions, independent trade unionism does not exist.

As far as we are aware, no such map has previously been attempted. The categories and definitions were determined on the advice of leading international trade union officials. Although the first two categories divide states into those where independent trade unions comprise more than and less than half the labour force, it was not our intention to quantify in detail the numbers of workers in trade unions. In fact, in the United Kingdom for instance, almost half of all employed workers are in unions and the trend is upwards. In the United States, for comparison, only about a quarter of the workforce is unionized and the proportion is declining.

Trade unions that are totally controlled, as in the USSR, Eastern Europe and a number of Asian and African states, are essentially organs of government with no independence of decision. Trade unions that are tightly controlled, as in many other African states, have independence of decision in form, but are in fact permitted such independence only when there is no conflict with major government policies.

There was some disagreement between trade union experts on the appropriate category for trade unionism in certain African states, such as Zambia, Nigeria, Ghana and Kenya and also others in Latin America.

42. The Force of Labour

This map compares the incomes of the top 5 per cent in individual states, with the bottom 20 per cent. Although the statistics used relate to the sixties and the early seventies, no later information was available.

The disparity is large, but in reality may be even greater. For a number of reasons, the incomes of the rich are systematically understated by the statistics. It is now widely recognized that the rich enjoy various forms of consumption outside the expenditure of their official after-tax incomes. In Western capitalist societies and their imitators elsewhere, executives, for instance, are provided with forms of untaxed income in kind: the use of company-owned apartments, cars and even

43. Rich and Poor People

planes; participation in company-subsidized schemes for private medical treatment and the private education of children; and a whole multitude of minor benefits which can be broadly described as expense-account entertainment. In addition, instead of salary increases which bring with them a high rate of tax, they are frequently offered option and other equity allowances likely to produce a capital gain and be taxed at a much lower rate, if at all.

Although figures are not available for incomes in the USSR and Eastern Europe, bureaucrats there also have access to privileged consumption beyond their official incomes: through state-supplied living quarters and transport, special medical facilities, special schools or places at schools, and their own shops which make available rare or subsidized goods.

The inset map shows the dramatic division between rich and poor within groups of economies determined by its source, UNCTAD, and which includes Yugoslavia among the 'developed market economies' and Cuba among the 'developed centrally planned' ones.

44. Our Daily Bread

This map shows the number of calories available per head of population in each state and the incidence of famines between 1950 and 1979.

The minimum calorie intake, as defined by the World Health Organization, takes into account climatic conditions, types of work, sex and average weight, and has been incorporated into the figures on which this map is based.

The most extreme cases of states with mass calorie deprivation correspond with the Sahel region of West Africa which suffered severe drought and famine between 1972 and 1974 and which reached their peak in 1973. The Sahel drought is illustrated in the inset map.

Although some rich states, such as Canada, West Germany and Sweden, appear to be less privileged than the USSR and Czechoslovakia, it should be remembered that calorie intake is the most simple of food measures. The diet of the former may involve a higher intake of protein, vitamins and other food values.

The following table provides comparative information on protein deficiency. It appeared in the Food and Agricultural Organization's *Fourth World Survey*, 1977.

state	year of survey	age group (in years)	% suffering from protein energy malnutrition		
			Severe	Moderate	Total
India		1–5	2.0	52.7	54.7
Rwanda	1971	0–5	9.8	44.9	54.7
Cameroon	1973	0–5	4.4	36.4	40.8
Cen. Af. Rep.	1972	0–5	3.0	36.4	39.4
Guatemala	1967	0–4	5.9	26.5	32.4
Guyana	1971	0–4	1.3	30.8	32.1
Haiti	1971	0–5	6.0	25.0	31.0
Burundi	1972	0–5	2.2	28.7	30.4
El Salvador	1967	0–4	3.1	22.9	26.0
Kenya	1968		1.0	25.0	26.0
Brazil	1970	0–4	6.3	18.9	25.2
Colombia	1968		1.7	19.3	21.0
Jamaica	1970	0–3	1.4	18.0	19.4
Barbados	1969	0–4	1.2	15.3	16.5
Venezuela	1971	1–6	0.9	14.5	15.4

For Barbados, El Salvador, Guatemala, Guyana, Jamaica and Venezuela, these were national samples; for Cameroon, the sample was limited to Douala; for the remainder, no further details are given.

Protein deficiency is permanently damaging to small children since it affects the development of the brain.

During the Sahel famine 1972–74, whole populations were uprooted and people died in hundreds of thousands. Exceptionally low rainfall had aggravated the cumulative effects of unrestrained grazing, excessive cultivation and short-sighted social policies.

Early reports suggest that the current famine (1980) in East Africa, the result of civil conflict and war, as well as agricultural neglect and inadequate rainfall, may claim even more victims.

Susan George, citing a National Geographic magazine report of a satellite photograph of the Sahel region, provides a useful correction to the 'climatic' explanation for the tragedy. The photograph shows 'a hexagonal island of green in the tan sea of the Sahel. Inspection revealed it to be a quarter-million acre modern ranch, fenced off with barbed-wire from the surrounding desert. Inside, other fences divide the ranch into five sectors, with cattle grazing a single sector at a time. Though the ranch has been in operation only seven years, the rotational grazing has made the difference between pasture and desert. (Susan George, *How the Other Half Dies: The Real Reasons for World Hunger*, Penguin 1976, page 45.)

45. Bill of Health

This map shows infant mortality rates, life expectancy figures for both men and women and also the number of hospital beds in proportion to population.

Infant mortality is the single most important factor in the measurement of life expectancy at birth and a high rate of infant mortality will reduce significantly figures for life expectancy.

Incidence of hospital beds as an index of medical provision should not be taken to imply a judgement on the value of Western allopathic medicine compared with traditional homeopathic systems. There is no means of telling the extent of provision of traditional systems of medicine, and therefore no way of using them for international comparison; and Western medicine is internationally dominant.

46. The Right to Learn

This map shows the extent of illiteracy in individual states. It also shows the percentage enrolment of the population of appropriate age in primary, secondary and tertiary education. In some states, children of secondary school age are still at primary schools, thus inflating the percentage in primary education and reducing the percentage in secondary education. In Gabon, the Lebanon and Hong Kong for example, this pushes the primary school figure to above 100 per cent.

The limited resources that poor states are able to devote to higher education are in many cases ultimately diverted abroad (see *Map 20: Technological Power* and *Map 38: The Flight to Work*), or into the service of local subsidiaries of transnational corporations whose profits are exported (see *Map 36: The Nationality of Transnationals*). What remains is often the more irrelevant for being too closely modelled on imported curricula which reflect the needs and conditions of alien societies. The predictable result is a high drop-out rate and the explosive resentment that go with it.

47. The Longer Reach

There are few ways in which the citizen can reach out from immediate circumstances to give and receive news, ideas and opinions, in exchanges which constitute the vital source of intellectual emancipation and which so many governments see as a challenge and even a threat. The two such instruments chosen are the telephone, an essentially private form of communication, and newsprint, essentially a means of public communication.

It is certainly true that in many societies poverty is principally responsible for the lack of both. But, as the map reveals, there are some states, the Soviet Union for example, where neither economic backwardness nor widespread illiteracy can explain the relatively small number of telephones available or the relatively low consumption of newsprint.

Of course, newsprint consumption levels can give no indication of who owns or controls the press, or show degrees of press freedom. Nor does access to a telephone guarantee private and free communication.

48. Holes in the Safety Net

This map shows the percentage of welfare payments made by states to individuals, as a percentage of gross domestic product. The data for the map have been taken from the eighth and ninth international inquiries into *The Cost of Social Security*, conducted by the International Labour Office and covering the years 1971–74 in the eighth inquiry and 1976–1979 in the ninth inquiry. Most data comes from the ninth inquiry, except in the case of fourteen states.

A comparison of the results of the two inquiries confirms the truth of that most uncharitable of injunctions 'to those who have, let more be given'. Where comparison between 1971 and 1974 was possible, the proportion of net welfare receipts to gross domestic product fell in every state in Africa, every state in Asia apart from Japan; and every state in South America, except for oil-rich Venezuela. The proportion rose only in Oceania, and throughout Europe except for Czechoslovakia and Greece.

49. The Swelling Cities

This map deals with the internal migration of people. It shows that in most states there is a persistent net migration of country dwellers to towns and cities. Since the total populations of all states except East Germany have increased (see *Map 3: The State by Population*) this has usually been accompanied by a less significant rise in rural population. In East Germany both urban and rural populations have declined, partly as a result of large-scale migration to West Germany in the period before the Berlin Wall was built. In Western and Eastern Europe and North America there has been an actual decline in rural population and this is shown on the map.

A UN monitoring report, *World Population Trends and policies 1977*, 1979, has compared the attitudes of various governments towards population distribution between cities and countryside and the policies pursued.

Out of the 146 governments surveyed, 112 regarded the rate of urbanization as either 'substantially unacceptable' or 'extremely unacceptable'. Yet only 80 of these claim to have policies directed at decelerating – not reversing – the process and 16 had policies of no intervention whatsoever.

The survey produced some strange anomalies. Bhutan and Cyprus regarded their spatial distribution as 'slightly unacceptable', Brazil and Saudi Arabia as 'substantially unacceptable', yet all four were pursuing policies of 'acceleration' of urban growth. On the other hand, East Germany, Hungary, Czechoslovakia and Sweden regarded their spatial distribution as 'entirely acceptable', while at the same time they were pursuing attempts to decelerate the process.

50. Slumland

This map uses access to safe water supplies as the most unambiguous index available of urban health. Other indices, such as area of floor space per person or the number of people per room or dwelling unit are clearly open to misinterpretation when compared internationally.

The map also shows percentage areas of slums in many of the world's major cities. Since the source of information was the United Nations *Second World Housing Survey*, 1974, the most recent available, and only selected cities were included, there appear to be obvious omissions: perhaps Kingston (Jamaica), Port of Spain (Trinidad), La Paz (Bolivia), Jakarta (Indonesia) and Soweto (South Africa) – to name but a few examples. And since economic growth rates are now declining almost everywhere, and the proportion of slum dwellers in the urban population was increasing even in the period of high economic growth, it is reasonable to assume that the situation today is substantially worse than is conveyed by the map.

This map deals with criminal activity as defined by state authorities and also with murder as the supreme human crime. Definitions of crime are obviously open to varieties of interpretation by individual states but in general all crimes which come to the attention of the police, other than traffic offences, are included. Murder is defined as any act performed (successfully) with the intention of taking human life. This definition excludes manslaughter and abortion, but not infanticide.

The fact that statistics can be very misleading is exemplified by definitions of crime in South Africa. There are serious crimes in South Africa which would not be regarded as crimes at all by other states, notably sexual relations between members of different races as defined by South Africa's Immorality Act. Figures for murder, while high, are in reality much higher still, since murders within the black community are sometimes not brought to the attention of the police. And although the numbers may be numerically marginal, statistics for murder do not include those who have died under police interrogation from allegedly natural causes. The peculiarly high figure for murder in the Lebanon may be explained by the escalating political violence that preceded the civil war.

The principal source of statistics used for this map, the International Criminal Police Organization (Interpol) offers some words of caution:

'The General Secretariat simply reproduces the information given on the forms from each country . . . The information . . . is unsophisticated but uniform . . .

'We emphasize the fact that the data given in this report is [sic] in no way intended to be used as a basis for comparison between different countries. Our statistics cannot take account of the differences which exist between the definitions of what constitutes an indictable offence in the various national legislatures considered, of the different methods of calculation, nor of any changes in legal definitions, the structure of the various services engaged in criminal investigation and the conditions under which it is carried out, which may have occurred during the period covered by the report. Bearing in mind all these unknown factors, together with others which influence police investigation, the figures which appear in this report must be considered approximate and should therefore be interpreted with great caution.'

We felt compelled to abandon our original plan for a map on recent rates of unemployment throughout the world for reasons explained in the Introduction.

This chart is taken from one produced by the International Labour Office in 1974. It uses current UN population projections and a rule-of-thumb correlation between total population and economically active population, to present the likely profile of unemployment in rich and poor states up to the year 2150.

Such projections are frequently subject to sudden amendment or refinement which may be caused by new evidence or even new theories. And the chart itself is clearly based on economic trends in the past that may well not be reflected in the future. The difficulties and instabilities of the present world economic system (see Maps 55–59 in particular) point to a period of much slower economic growth than has been known since the second world war, if not to a period of stagnation or even contraction. Such a period, if significantly prolonged, would significantly reduce the economically active proportion to the whole.

At the very least, this chart warns of the blighted future that could affect many millions of lives.

Given the reluctance of the world's states to acknowledge the damage being done to its most basic resources, this map can evoke only some of the worst known examples of pollution to air and sea.

Sea pollution is a phenomenon more recognized than measured. Therefore the map, though based on the data available, remains essentially impressionistic and concentrates on those areas known to be most heavily affected.

In the Mediterranean, the problem has reached emergency dimensions and more detailed information is available which is shown in the inset map. But in addition to the pollutants included, there are at least two other major industrial sources of pollution in the Mediterranean: mercury waste and pesticides.

Air pollution is shown by two limited regional studies of the most commonly dangerous industrial pollutants: sulphur dioxide, which becomes sulphuric acid when combined with water vapour and which is a prime cause of chronic lung disease; and lead, which can seriously and permanently damage the nervous system and is particularly dangerous for children.

It is important to emphasize that pollution is neither local nor isolated. For this reason individual, though dramatic, instances of pollution disasters, such as the mercury poisoning at Minimata (Japan), first officially identified in 1956, and the dioxin poisoning in Seveso (Italy) in 1976 have not been included.

54. The Dying Earth

The purpose of this map is to demonstrate not only the steady increase in desert across the earth, but also the part played in this increase by neglect and deliberate injury.

The map identifies bioclimatic zones, shows areas where there is very high or moderate risk of intensifying or extending aridity and some of the major causes. Vulnerable land includes stony or rocky surfaces, areas subject to soil stripping and gully erosion, areas subject to sand movement, and land with excess salt or bad soil structure. Human and animal pressure refers to density of human population and livestock. Human pressure also includes intense pressure of cultivation associated with mechanization.

It has taken thousands of years for large tracts of desert and semi-desert land to develop out of what were once fertile regions: years in which haphazard human encroachment has upset the delicate balance on which ecological renewal depends.

In recent years this encroachment has become more violent. In large parts of Africa for example, population pressure, patterns of land ownership and war have intensified the destruction of land, increased blight to a virtually endemic condition and produced almost permanent famine (see *Map 44: Our Daily Bread*).

Technology has made possible more deliberate large-scale encroachment and drastic changes in land use can be effected. Vast tracts of rain forest in Brazil are now being turned into grazing land, creating a potential desert of the future.

The extension of desert and arid zones has more than local and regional significance. Large-scale changes in land patterns and use can have major effects on both the weather and the renewal of the world's oxygen supply.

In times of war, even more powerful techniques of destruction are employed, and employed deliberately. The inset map shows the extent of war pollution in Vietnam, Kampuchea and Laos. Whole regions have been poisoned and destroyed through the spraying of herbicides and defoliants and bombardment with shrapnel.

The report of the UN Conference on Desertification 1977, concluded that although more than one-third of the earth's land is already arid, declining fertility and productivity, caused by current levels of intensification, will affect the livelihood of well over 600 million people, most of whom live in poor states.

55. Industrial Droop

This map introduces a section on the emerging symptoms of crisis within the world economic system. What it shows specifically is the decline in the growth rates of industrial production between the sixties and the seventies – a decline which continues to accelerate.

The causes are both complex and arguable. The consequences are momentous (see, for example, *Map 56: The First Inflationary Crest, 1974; Map 59: Panic Stations* and *Map 65: Urban Heavings in the Seventies*).

56. The First Inflationary Crest, 1974

There is no more effective form of undermining the social order than through the unexpected and apparently remedyless inequities induced by a high and rising cost of inflation. In so far as there is a single dominant symptom of crisis in the world system, it is precisely this problem of inflation, which governments freely acknowledge but are patently unable to solve.

A huge rise in the price of oil was made by OPEC in September 1973. But this was itself in large measure a response to the surge of inflation from the end of the sixties. By 1971, world inflation was running at an annual 6.6 per cent, and by 1973 at an annual 9.5 per cent. In 1974, it reached 15.1 per cent overall. In some states, notably the United Kingdom, inflation did not crest until 1975, but in the majority of states, inflation had done so in the previous year.

Figures for inflation are not provided by the Soviet Union or states in Eastern Europe. But if the rates of inflation there were, as claimed, lower than in the industrial West, this was at least in part because consumer queues were appreciably longer.

That the world inflationary crisis in 1974 was no isolated pheno-menon is already evident. There was a further inflationary surge in the late seventies, a surge that had not yet crested at the start of 1980. At the end of 1979, inflation figures in many states, notably in such major industrial ones as the USA, Canada and the United Kingdom, were already running above the rate in 1974.

57. Funny Money

Whatever the causes of inflation, there can be no doubt that significant among them is a substantial rise in the supply of money, unmatched by a rise in the production of goods and services.

This map shows the growth in the money supply in individual states over a ten-year period, 1968–77. The figures for a few states do not cover the full ten years, because the statistical series of which they were a part changed their bases during the period. Figures for the United States, the dominant state in the world monetary system, appear peculiarly low. But alongside this low increase in the domestic supply of dollars, there was a massive increase in the supply of expatriate dollars, primarily located in what is known as the Euro-dollar market (see *Map 58: Credit Runs Riot*).

The inset map shows how far the purchasing power of the major currencies was eroded between 1950 and 1975.

58. Credit Runs Riot

If inflation is one symptom of increasing economic instability (see *Map 56: The First Inflationary Crest, 1974*) another is the enormous and accelerating growth of credit. The trend to economic crisis is intensified when such credit rises are accompanied by levels of industrial produc-tion and gross national product which are in retreat (see *Map 55: Industrial Droop* and *Map 23: National Income*).

Almost all states and international agencies have participated in the scramble for credit. But while some have been able to borrow on the basis of their conspicuous ability to repay (OPEC member states), others (non-OPEC 'developing' states) have been given further credit because of their very inability to meet current obligations.

Most have been accommodated on the Euro-currency market, the fastest growing international credit market and the one least subject to state surveillance and controls. This map shows recent expansion in Euro-currency bank credits which is measured by the foreign currency liabilities of banks in major European states and in the Bahamas, Cayman

Islands, Bahrain, Panama, Japan, Canada, Hong Kong and Singapore.

The Euro-currency market is essentially the market in money held outside its state of origin. About 75 per cent of this market is in expatriate US dollars and the growth in this element has been some ten times the growth in the US domestic money supply during the seventies. This enormous increase in the Euro-dollar sector, with an average annual rate of around 70 per cent in the last decade, has been a primary cause of international credit growth and inflation.

The high and rising cost of credit is shown in the inset map. This is measured as the 'prime rate', or rate of interest charged to best customers, of commercial banks. It is a product of inflation and also a contributory cause, since it often makes borrowing for investment purposes prohibitively expensive and contracts the base of industrial production (see *Map 55: Industrial Droop*).

59. Panic Stations

As a result of the problems depicted in Maps 55–58, there has been an increasing flight from the paper currencies into gold.

The main map shows some of the different features of the gold market: it shows gold producers and levels of gold production; it shows gold holdings of individual states and identified private hoarding; it shows the extent of gold bullion movements throughout the world; and in a graph it shows the annual average increase in the free market price of gold since 1968.

The map indicates the central role played by Switzerland in the world gold market. It is a role essentially supported by special arrangements between leading Swiss banks and the South African Reserve Bank, arrangements which did much to reduce the importance of London, once the centre of the international gold market.

Figures for the Soviet Union's gold production and gold holdings are not made public; but gold production is generally estimated at almost 13 million ounces and holdings have been reported to be over 63 million ounces.

In March 1978, the gold holdings of states within the European Monetary System dropped by almost 20 per cent when corresponding contributions were made to its central pool. Private hoarding is almost invariably secret. We have included estimates by Consolidated Gold Fields for the principal private hoards known to exist in France and India. We have added a Bundesbank estimate for accumulated purchases of Krugerrands (South African gold coins weighing one ounce) in West Germany.

In the United States, it became legal for private citizens to hold and deal in gold at the end of 1974, and this has become a major factor in the international gold market. An even more direct and substantial impact has been made by the New York and Chicago markets in gold futures — contracts to buy or sell specified amounts of gold for a certain price and at a certain date.

Net sales from official monetary gold stocks to private purchasers have consisted in recent years almost entirely of sales from the International Monetary Fund and from the US Treasury. Such sales, at 11.67 million ounces, do not necessarily all find their way into private stocks, since some may have been additions to the gold holdings of certain central banks.

The inset map shows how the flight into gold has been accompanied by a similar movement from the weaker to the stronger currencies.

60. Nuclear Power, No Thanks

By the year 2000, it has been estimated, there will be more than a hundred nuclear power plants which are no longer operational. In addition, there will be hundreds of smaller nuclear installations — research accelerators, fuel enrichment and reprocessing plants, naval reactors, nuclear medical facilities — whose productive lives are at an end. All of them will remain radioactive for hundreds or even thousands of years: an ever-present danger to future generations.

Opposition to nuclear power has taken various forms. In Japan and Yugoslavia, for instance, it is done primarily by law-suit. In some states it has merged into the wider political process. In Sweden, during 1976, it was material in bringing more than four decades of social democratic government to an end. And elsewhere, too, the ballot box has been used to notable effect. In Austria, Denmark, parts of Belgium and parts of the United States, the encroachment of nuclear power has been arrested or slowed by referendum. In other states such as the Soviet Union and Eastern Europe, it is part of a political debate conducted behind closed doors.

The public opposition shown in this map encompasses direct action protests against the whole nuclear energy industry: from uranium mining to the trade in reactors and methods of disposal of nuclear waste. Direct action is shown in all its forms: from industrial strikes and sabotage, demonstrations and festivals, to confrontation and battles with the police. If anything, the extent of such activity is likely to be understated: major West European and American newspapers, which are the source of information for the map, may not have reported many protests which were either small, spontaneous or hidden by authority.

What the map cannot show is the international character of the protest movement: the contingents of Danish protesters in Germany and Sweden; of Germans in France and Switzerland; of French in Germany; of British in France — a character that is a recognition of the degree to which a nuclear facility in one state can affect the environment in another.

Where action has been widespread, as on the Hiroshima—Nagasaki commemoration days of August 1977 in the United States, or the rail transport strike of May 1976 in Australia, symbols have been sited in the appropriate national or regional capital city.

While we had intended to indicate all sites of nuclear accidents grave enough to lead to a shutdown of a nuclear facility, there were so few plants *not* affected that the map would have been rendered meaningless. This strongly confirmed our view that the everyday technical operation of all nuclear facilities is highly dangerous.

61. Nationalism Against the Nation State

One powerful manifestation of dissent against the current world system is the existence of a wide variety of movements seeking to revise either boundaries or allegiances. While they are not all necessarily beneficial, they reflect some of the irrationalities in the world's division into states and in some cases suggest that there may be further proliferation (see *Map 2: The Proliferation of States* and the corresponding note).

Separatist movements seek to create a new state out of one or more already established. Irridentist movements seek a readjustment of state frontiers. Regionalist movements seek to achieve some or more autonomy within their established state. We have been forced to make our own judgements about these movements and have coded the information into easily understood shorthand descriptions.

All movements have been classified as either active or dormant. An active movement is one whose activities have evoked a significant response from authority, usually involving police or army action of some kind. A dormant movement is one considered to have been active within the last ten years or so, which may well become active again, but which was not active at the end of the seventies.

Such definitions inevitably encompass wide variations. The separatist movement in Wales, however serious its intentions, is at present little more than a source of irritation to the government of the United Kingdom. Whereas the separatist movements of the Kurds have involved more than one established state in protracted warfare and remain a major source of conflict in the region.

The current armed struggle in Namibia is defined as separatist, since it is primarily directed to ending that country's effective integration with South Africa. But since Namibia has always been a separate territory, whose independence is recognized by the United Nations and its member states, including recently South Africa itself, its struggle is less a manifestation of separatism than a national rebellion against an occupying foreign power.

The government of Taiwan, like the government of China, claims Taiwan to be an integral part of China. In this context, there is a Taiwanese separatist commitment in the Formosan Independence Movement.

We have not attempted to depict the complex situation in the USSR in this map. For this, see *Map 62: Russia's Ununited Republics.*

62. Russia's Ununited Republics

In a state as centralized, diverse and extensive as the USSR, nationalist challenges are inevitable though repressed. Challenge to state control, and to the dominance of the Russian republic within the USSR, date back to the resistance of the Georgian people to incorporation during 1921–22. This event was directly responsible for the conflict between Lenin and Stalin at the end of Lenin's active political life. Stalin won the day and ever since, the Russian government – we use the word 'Russian' advisedly – has reacted with consistent ferocity to crush any movement for or towards national self-determination.

Despite propaganda and education, as well as more brutal methods of repression, nationalist movements have continually emerged, not least among the peoples of the 'annihilated' republics: the five Autonomous Soviet Socialist Republics or ASSRs (Crimean, Chechen-Ingush, Kabardino-Balkar, Kalmyk, and Volga German) and the Karachay Autonomous Region. All of these disappeared from official maps of the Soviet Union in the early years of the second world war and their entire populations were deported to Soviet Central Asia. Four of them (Chechen-Ingush, Kabardino-Balkar and Kalmyk ASSRs and the Karachay AR) were restored in 1957.

Information on resistance movements in the USSR is necessarily scant and uncertain and distinctions between levels of activity must be a matter of judgement. In gathering material for this map, we have called upon a number of experts and a large variety of sources, including oblique references in official reports.

The psychiatric 'hospitals' identified on this map are used for the punishment and control of political dissent. They are administered not by the Ministry of Health but by the Ministry of the Interior.

63. 'Our Bodies Our Selves'

A central theme of the women's liberation movement is the need for women to take charge of their own fates, a right widely denied them by the male-dominated societies of our world. The most satisfactory measure we have found for its success in this respect is contained in this map on abortion rights.

The map shows the spread in legal provisions: from states in which the right to abortion is denied women altogether, to states in which there is some recognition that women should have the right to decide for themselves. In most states there is some right to abortion, but on more or less restricted criteria, and by leave of some, predominantly male, authority.

In no state is the right to abortion a woman's own. Even in the Netherlands, possibly the most liberal in practice, abortion on demand is available only in non-profit clinics; with formal legal sanction for abortion only on narrow medical grounds. In Cuba, another liberal state, abortion on demand is available in government hospitals. Both the Netherlands and Cuba have been put in the most liberal category.

Where abortion is available on demand for certain groups of women only, the criteria differ widely. They include age (usually women over forty); the number of living children (the number varies); and even, in Hungary, whether women have a home of their own. Where abortion is permitted within a specified time limit, that limit is usually the first ten to twelve weeks of pregnancy, as in most of Eastern Europe, but can be as little as eight weeks (Sweden) or as much as twenty-four weeks (Singapore).

Very often, legal provision and social practice are wide apart. France, while fairly liberal in theory, is restrictive in practice; in the Philippines, the opposite is true.

The definitions used need explanation: 'social or social-medical grounds' cover the well-being of the woman and her existing family; 'juridical grounds' cover rape and incest; 'broad medical and eugenic grounds' cover abortion granted to safeguard a woman's physical health and to prevent the transmission of incurable hereditary diseases; 'narrow medical grounds' cover only cases where a woman's life is at stake. We have taken 'social or social-medical grounds' to be a broader category than 'medical, juridical or eugenic grounds' and have adopted it as the determining one where both are given.

In some states with a federal system of government, national legal provisions are moderated by state law and range from extreme liberality (California in the US, Slovenia in Yugoslavia, and South Australia) to extreme restrictiveness (Louisiana in the US, Queensland in Australia).

The inset map shows changing official attitudes to abortion and draws attention to the danger that liberal trends can be reversed where women are not in full control of the decision on abortion. Many East European states, for example, having induced women to enter the labour force by making abortions freely available after the second world war, are now trying to reverse the consequent decline in new entrants to the labour force and the armed services by making abortion more difficult to obtain.

64. The Student Sixties

The student unrest that so spectacularly characterized the closing two years of the sixties was not a new phenomenon. A prominently student opposition to government policy has been endemic in many parts of the world since the second world war; notably in Latin America. Students were in the forefront of the British Campaign for Nuclear Disarmament in the early sixties; were leading militants of the Civil Rights Movement in the United States; and staged, in 1964, on the Berkeley campus of the University of California, a revolt that served as the prototype and pre-cursor of hundreds that took place across the world before the end of the decade.

The student upheavals in each country may be traced to particular conditions or events. In France, it was the sclerotic inflexibility of the Gaullist educational — and political — regime. In West Germany, earlier, in 1967, it was a state visit by the Shah of Iran and the harshness with which his security was protected. In the United States, it was the Vietnam war and the associated demands of the draft. But although there were, everywhere, particular issues and circumstances, there was also a sense of unity that encouraged protest to leap from one campus to another and from one country to another, in a remarkable international movement that was always dramatic and occasionally, as in France and the United States, so important as radically to alter the political scene.

In promoting this sense of unity, an instrument of undoubted influence was the rapid communication of events, by press, radio, and, most vividly, television. But there was too, an underlying unity of dis-content, at educational regimes which processed rather than educated the huge numbers of students resulting from the university expansion of the preceding period, and which provided degrees without acceptable opportunities of employment.

We have defined student disruptions as any student demonstrations that interrupted the normal course of teaching or administration and which led to outside intervention. In a few states, there were disruptions in sites so close together — as at various universities within Tokyo — that they could not be depicted separately on the map. We have identified 89 individual sites in the United States, 37 in Japan, and 32 in Pakistan. Finally, we found no way of singling out sites of repeated student disruption, without causing confusion.

65. Urban Heavings in the Seventies

Urban disorders were no more peculiar to the seventies than student disruptions to the end of the sixties (see *Map 64: The Student Sixties*). But just as student disruption in 1968–69 was remarkable for its extent and its impact, so urban disorder in the seventies reached an unprecedented incidence and intensity.

Some common factors can be identified: both were promoted by improved communications and especially by television; both were prompted by particular incidents, conditions or circumstances in their state of origin; but again, in both there was an underlying unity of impulse, emanating here from increased urbanization (see *Map 50: The Swelling Cities*) alongside a general decline in economic growth. While there was no corresponding increase in employment opportunities (see *Map 55: Industrial Droop* and *Map 52: The Unemployment Time Bomb*), there was an explosive increase in areas of urban deprivation (see *Map 49: Slumland*) accompanied by pressures from inflation (see *Map 56: The First Inflationary Crest, 1974*), especially on the lives of the poor.

An urban upheaval is defined as an urban disorder sufficiently serious in intensity or extent to involve intervention of the authorities by force. Industrial action has been included where it reflects social revolt rather than specific strikes over wages or working conditions. Urban upheavals which have led to a change in government policy or of the government itself are indicated on the site of the national or regional capital.

Subject Index

Abortion 63
Advertising 19
Agricultural workers 40
Air force bases 7
Aircraft 10
Air pollution 53
Antarctica 4
Antimony 13
Arid zones 54
Armies 29
Arms supply 11
Army bases 7

Bank lending rates 58
Banks, assets 35
Bauxite 13

Calories 44
Chrome 13
Coal 15
Combat aircraft 10
Conscientious objection 30
Conscription 30
Copper 13
Credit 58
Crime 51
Currencies, major 57, 59

Death penalty 31
Debt, external public 24
    and export income 24
Deserts and desertification
    54
Diamonds 13
Drug industry 36

Education 46
Energy consumption/
    production 15
Engineers 20
Euro-currencies 58
Exclusive Economic Zones 5
Exploitation 39
Export income 21
Export trade 22

Famines 44
Fishing disputes 5
Flags of convenience 37
Food, availability of 44
Food trade 18
Foreign currency reserves
    25, 35
Free production zones 37

Gold bullion movements 59
Gold hoarding, private 59
Gold prices 59
Gold production 59
Gold reserves 25, 35, 59
Government income 26
Gross domestic product
    and government income 26

and military spending 8
    and welfare receipts 48
Gross national product 23,25

Health 45
Housing 50

Industrial growth 55
Industrial output 19
Industrial workers 40
Infant mortality 45
Inflation 56
Internal security forces 27
Imports 25
Iron 14
Irridentist movements 61

Languages 33
Lead 13
Life expectancy 45
Literacy 46

Manganese 13
Manufacturing output 19
Martial law 28
Medical provision 45
Migrant workers 38
    brain drain 20
Military bases 7
Military expenditure 8
Military regimes 28
Military service 30
Mineral resources 13, 14
Money supply 57
Monoculture 21
Multinationals see
    Transnationals
Murder 51

Nationalist movements 61,
    62
Naval bases 7
Newsprint consumption 47
Nickel 13
Nuclear power 17
    protests against 60
Nuclear weapons 9
    protests against 60

Offshore manufacturing
    zones 37
Oil movements 16
Oil production 16
OPEC 16

People's militias 27
Pharmaceutical industry 36
Police 27
Political prisoners 31
Pollution 53
Population 2, 3
    and incomes 43
    and unemployment 52

Public administration
    workers 27

Religions 34
Rural population 49
Russia 62
Refugees 32
Regionalist movements 61

Sahel, drought 44
Satellites 6
Scientists 20
Sea pollution 53
Separatist movements 61
Service workers 27
Sexual discrimination 41
Silver 14
Slums 50
Soldiers 29
Student disruptions 64

Tax havens 37
Teachers 46
Technology 20
Telephones 47
Tin 14
Torture 31
Trade 21, 22
    exports 21, 22
    imports 25
Trade unions 42

Unemployment 52
Uranium production and
        reserves 14
Uranium mining, protests
        against 60
Urban disorder 65
Urban population 49
Urban slums 50
USSR 62

War 12
War pollution 54
Water supply 50
Welfare receipts 48
Women
    abortion 63
    sexual discrimination in
        jobs 41
    workers 41
Worker migrants 38
    brain drain 20
Workers
    in agriculture 40
    in industry 40
    in public administration 27
    women 41

Zinc 14